MEDIUM ÆVUM MONOGRAPHS
NEW SERIES V

THE LYRICS OF THE

RED BOOK OF OSSORY

Edited by

RICHARD LEIGHTON GREENE

The Society for the Study of Medieval
Languages and Literature, Oxford

THE SOCIETY FOR THE STUDY OF
MEDIEVAL LANGUAGES AND LITERATURE

http://mediumaevum.modhist.ox.ac.uk

© Richard Leighton Greene, 1974

First published for the Society for the Study of Mediæval
Languages and Literature, by Basil Blackwell, Oxford, 1974

This digital reprint, with minor typological
corrections, first issued 2015

ISBN-13: 978-0-907570-69-1 (pb)

PREFACE

In addition to the acknowledgements made in the text of the introduction, I am happy to record the advice, encouragement, and assistance of Professor J.A.W. Bennett of Magdalene College, Cambridge, of Dr. John Stevens of the same college, and of my former student, Joy Day Buel. Parts of the introduction, with adaptations, have been read before Group English II of the Modern Language Association of America and the Oxford Medieval Society.

My greatest obligation has been to the late Bishop of Ossory, Ferns and Leighlin, the Right Reverend John Percy Phair, not only for permission to transcribe and publish these sixty poems but also for friendly interest and gracious hospitality during my study of the manuscript at the Palace in Kilkenny.

Richard Leighton Greene

Note on the texts: Emendation has been kept to a minimum. Expanded abbreviations are underlined. Capitalisation, punctuation, and word-division follow modern usage. The English letter w occurring in Latin texts has been printed as uu.

THE LYRICS OF THE RED BOOK OF OSSORY

The Red Book of Ossory, so named from its medieval binding of crimson leather, is kept today, as it has been for centuries, in the Bishop's Palace in the picturesque city of Kilkenny. It contains official copies of many documents of the diocese of Ossory ranging in date from the early fourteenth century to the sixteenth. Although the volume was described and a facsimile of one page was published some ninety years ago, it has not yet been closely studied. [1] A full century has elapsed since a correspondent of Notes and Queries briefly mentioned the existence in the Red Book of sixty Latin poems, to some of which are prefixed scraps of Old French and Middle English verse, and surmised correctly that these fragments designate the popular airs to which the Latin verses were designed to be sung. [2] From time to time writers on the medieval lyric have noticed these bits of vernacular song more or less perfunctorily, and a few have attempted further comments on them, usually without sight of the original manuscript. [3] Eleven of the Latin lyrics were published by Sir J.T. Gilbert in the Historical Manuscripts Commission Reports in 1885, but no edition of the whole series has been undertaken before the present one, which is published by the kind permission of the late Bishop of Ossory, Ferns and Leighlin.

The Red Book itself is a folio, 12 1/8 by 8 7/8 inches over the binding, containing 79 vellum leaves generally 11 3/4 by 8 1/2 inches, though many are of irregular size and a few have damaged margins. One leaf, f. 68, is a fragment. An 'Index Libri Rubri Ossor:' of the eighteenth century on four paper leaves is inserted in the front. The manuscript is bound in oak boards covered with leather which has turned a dull mouse-gray on the outside but has kept its original rich strawberry-crimson dye where it has been protected from exposure. The pages of the book were used over many years for a succession of widely varied entries in at least thirty-six different hands, the latest items being of the reign of Queen Elizabeth I. Many of the prose articles are copies for record of documents

1. [Sir] John T. Gilbert, Historical Manuscripts Commission, Report X, Appendix, Part V (London, 1885), pp. 219-265; Facsimiles of the National Manuscripts of Ireland, Part IV, Vol. II (London, 1884), Appendix, Plate xxii. The lyrics printed by Gilbert are Nos. 9, 17, 28, 36, 37, 42, 43, 44, 45, 46, 60.
2. James Graves, First Series, II (1850), 385.
3. E.g. St. John D. Seymour, Anglo-Irish Literature 1200-1582 (Cambridge, 1929), 73-75, 96-98; R.H. Robbins, "The Earliest Carols and the Franciscans," Modern Language Notes, LIII (1938), 239-242; [Sir] E.K. Chambers, English Literature at the Close of the Middle Ages (Oxford, 1945), 81-82.

concerned with the business of the diocese. Two entries hold interest of
another kind. A two-page account in Latin of the exile of Thomas Becket
has been given the prescribed Reformation treatment of a wash of ink, which
not only fails to obliterate but for some reason stops short before the end of
the tract.[1] A long series of proverbs attributed to 'authorities' from Laban
and Nebuchednezzar to Seneca and 'the Sibyl' is carefully written in
rhymed quatrains of Old French and attests the full currency of that language
in the fourteenth-century cathedral community.[2]

The sixty lyrics here edited are found in the ten remaining leaves of
the last gathering of twelve, two leaves apparently having been removed
before the Latin verses were written. The condition of this last part of the
manuscript shows that the pages with the songs have been fingered many
times oftener than the rest of the volume. The lyrics are written in two
hands which do not appear elsewhere in the manuscript with the possible
exception that one of them may have written a short note prefixed to the
proverbs. The first of the hands has written ff. 70r.-75r. (column 1); the
second has written ff. 75r. (column 2)-77r. Both hands are of the later
fourteenth century but cannot be more exactly dated. The text of the
Latin pieces has been carefully corrected by someone who was not either
of the original scribes but who was nearly or quite contemporary with them.
The third hand has added the 'amen' to some pieces which lacked it.

The poems are neatly arranged in two columns to the page. At the
foot of the first page is the important memorandum, marked 'Nota', which
shows us that the songs result from the widespread impulse of churchmen to
replace irreligious songs with edifying ones:

      Attende, lector, q[uo]d Episcopus Ossoriensis
fecit istas cantilenas pro vicariis Ecclesie Cathedralis
sacerdotibus et clericis suis ad cantandum in magnis
festis et solaciis, ne guttura eorum et ora Deo sanctificata
polluantur cantilenis teatralibus, turpibus et secularibus,
et cum sint cantatores prouideant sibi de notis conuenientibus
secundum quod dictamina requirunt.

This may be translated as follows, with special care in the rendering of a
few key words:

---

1.   ff. 4r.-5r.
2.   ff. 66r.-67v.

Be advised, reader, that the Bishop of Ossory has
made these songs for the vicars of the cathedral church, for
the priests, and for his clerks, to be sung on the important
holidays and at celebrations (solaciis) in order that their
throats and mouths, consecrated to God, may not be polluted
by songs which are lewd, secular, and associated with revelry
(treatralibus), and, since they are trained singers (cantatores),
let them provide themselves with suitable tunes (notis) according
to what these sets of words (dictamina, 'ditties') require.

There can be no doubt that the Bishop of Ossory to whom the note
refers as the author of the songs is the famous Richard de Ledrede, who ruled
the see for nearly half of the fourteenth century, from his consecration at
Avignon in 1317 to his death in 1360. He was an Englishman, by his name
from Leatherhead in Surrey, though the chronicler Luke Wadding calls him
a Londoner by origin. [1] He was a Franciscan friar, like twenty-one other
Irish bishops of his century, and was trained at the same Franciscan house
in Canterbury which later produced the most copious of all known writers
of Middle English and macaronic carols, Brother James Ryman. [2]

The cathedral clergy whose consecrated throats were to sing these
lyrics were mostly, if not entirely, English. After Dublin, Kilkenny was the
most important centre of English power in Ireland and was surrounded by a
wall of legal privilege, outside of which the native Irish were zealously
kept. The present-day visitor to Kilkenny is reminded of this English
domination when he notices that one small part of the city is still known as
Irishtown and has a strong local feeling of its own. Medieval Kilkenny had
frequent contacts with the continent of Europe, especially with France, and
constant official intercourse with England. Its austerely beautiful cathedral
of St. Canice contains a few remains of the earlier Celtic church on the same
site, and the splendid round tower a few feet away from the cathedral
testifies to the ecclesiastical and strategic importance of the place before
the coming of the Normans. Bishop Richard de Ledrede's tomb is near the
high altar, but Cromwell's soldiers so efficiently destroyed the face of the
effigy upon it that we cannot tell today what he looked like, and there is
no other portrait of him. But there are abundant written records of his
tenure, which must have been a reign of terror for those whom he disliked.
He was a man of ability as well as of force and fanaticism, but so unruly that
he once had to be severely disciplined by the King. It appears likely that
before his death he became mentally deranged.

---

1. Luke Wadding, Scriptores Ordinis Minorum (Rome, 1906), p.203.
2. A.G. Little, Archaeologia Cantiana, LIV (1942), 2; Richard
    Leighton Greene, ed., A Selection of English Carols (Oxford, 1962),
    pp. 47-48.

The best known episode of his administration is his prosecution for witchcraft of Dame Alice Kyteler, a matron of one of the most respectable families of Kilkenny, and her associates. This sensational affair occurred in 1324, and a contemporary Latin account gives many circumstantial details which make it a document of prime importance in the history of witchcraft.[1] W. B. Yeats learned enough of it to be captivated by the account of Alice's familiar spirit, Robin Filius Artis, and he refers to it in the sombre finale of his poem Nineteen Hundred and Nineteen:

> But now wind drops, dust settles; thereupon
> There lurches past, his great eyes without thought
> Under the shadow of stupid straw-pale locks,
> That insolent friend Robert Artisson
> To whom the love-lorn Lady Kyteler brought
> Bronzed peacock feathers, red combs of her cocks.[2]

In the arrangement of the Latin poems in the manuscript some regard has obviously been had for their subject matter, and, while they are not in a completely systematic grouping, they are not written down in the haphazard order of some medieval collections. They include:

1. Twenty-five songs on the Nativity or closely related themes.

2. Eleven lyrics on Easter and the Resurrection, a continuous series coming directly after the large group of Nativity pieces.

3. A single song on the Annunciation.

4. Twenty-three pieces on diverse devotional subjects, the divisions between which, as in the manuscripts of English carols, are not always sharply drawn. Several of these, as will appear, are almost certainly not of Richard de Ledrede's original authorship.

The intention of the compiler or compilers to present the texts in a grouping based in part at least upon their association with particular feast days is shown by the headings of the first four pieces:

---

1. Thomas Wright, ed., A Contemporary Narrative of the Proceedings Against Dame Alice Kyteler, Camden Society, No. XXIV (London, 1843).
2. The Collected Poems of W. B. Yeats (London, 1952), p.237.

1.   Cantilena de Nativitate Domini

2.   Alia cantilena de eodem festo

3 and 4.   De eodem festo

The note about the Bishop's authorship follows the fourth song, and there are no such headings thereafter.

Allowing for the fact that some lyrics not regarded by a modern reader as 'Christmas songs' would be felt by the clerks of Kilkenny to be just as suitable for Christmas use as those which tell the Nativity story, we can safely conclude from the distribution in the Red Book that the Christmas season was in Kilkenny as in England the 'great feast' during which the custom of profane song most needed remedial attention. We can also conclude that Easter was next in this kind of importance, as would seem inherently probable. But the proposition of one Easter song to two Christmas songs is far higher than that in any manuscript collection of English carols and far higher than that in the corpus of all medieval English carols. Only sixteen of the 474 collected in my edition, The Early English Carols (Oxford, 1935), are specifically of the Passion or for Easter. The few carols found since its publication make no addition to this number. This is a striking contrast, and it is the deficiency of the English collections in Easter songs rather than the richness of the Red Book which challenges explanation.

The end of the anthology shows another conscious attempt at grouping. Here are found thirteen consecutive pieces which differ from the others less in their subjects than in their metres and literary style. Of this last baker's dozen ten are in metres quite unlike the markedly accentual and highly singable patterns of the first forty-seven. The whole group is much less suitable for singing to any tune associated with or derived from the dance. No. 53, in praise of the Virgin Mary, is a good example:

>   Concepit, peperit, intacta masculum,
>   Que nunquam masculi sencis opusculum,
>   Virtute celica;
>   Sic Deum efficit nostrum fraterculum
>   Nostra sorocula per carnis sacculum,
>   Beata viscera.
>
>   (Stanza 2)

Instead of being a literary exercise in paradox and diminutive, No. 59, a non-stanzaic piece for Christmas, shows obvious imitation of the responsorial parts of the service and must have been intended for music derived from the choir repertory rather than from the secular dance-songs of young people:

> Caritate nimia nos Deo diligente
>   Letemur hodie.
> Nato Dei filio de matre pariente
>   Letemur hodie.
> Verbum caro factum est, angelo docente,
>   Letemur hodie.
>   (etc.)

The last piece of all, No. 60, is even farther removed from any swing of the secular dance-song. It is a solemn exercise on the classical and medieval theme of Ubi sunt which is not unworthy to stand beside some of the best known treatments of that sobering rhetorical question. It has a stately repetend placed at the beginning and after each verse like a carol-burden, but there is nothing else about it that resembles a carol:

> Videbitis qualis et quantus mundi sit error in illecebris.
> Rectores habentes greges,
> Pomposi qui condunt leges,
>   Vbi iam sunt?
> Quorum gesta quia fuerunt
>   In latebris
> Velud funesta nunc perierunt
>   In tenebris.
>   (etc.)

No word of guidance or explanation concerning these latter texts is written in the manuscript, but internal evidence forces one to the conclusion that at or near the beginning of this group the memorandum about the Bishop's authorship ceases to apply. There is a change of hand after No. 42 which suggests the possibility of a change to a scribe or editor who simply went ahead and added to the Bishop's song-book any pious poetry of which he approved.

That Richard de Ledrede is not the author of all of the last thirteen pieces is made to appear more probable by the occurrence, not previously noticed in print, of portions of three of those pieces in two other unconnected manuscripts. On the other hand, diligent search has not found in any other source any of the lighter and more repetitive lyrics in the burden-and-stanza or refrain-stanza forms. In their case the Bishop's claim to originality is still unchallenged.

One of these three poems, No. 52, is representative of still another rhetorical style. It pursues to rather greater lengths than most modern tastes would approve the figure of Mary's baking in her oven the Bread of

Life, a figure conspicuously used by St. Thomas Aquinas.[1] Of the eight stanzas of No. 52, seven are also found in two successive unpublished poems in Bibliothèque Nationale MS 3757, f.60r., six of the stanzas (1, 3, 4, 2, 6, 7) in the first poem and one (8) in the second. This manuscript, of the fourteenth century and of English origin, contains works by John of Hoveden, the Yorkshire devotional poet of the later thirteenth century. The order of the stanzas and of a few lines differs in the Red Book from that of the Paris manuscript, and there are minor variant readings. The Paris texts were discovered by the late Dom André Wilmart, who very kindly sent me a copy through the late F.J.E. Raby, the editor of John of Hoveden's poems. Mr. Raby wrote that 'it seems' that they are the work of Richard de Ledrede, but believed that because of the differences in style from the first forty-seven lyrics of the Red Book it was wise to regard his authorship as doubtful unless some more definite evidence is found.[2] What is interestingly and positively indicated by this concordance is connection and communication between the important devotional literature of Yorkshire, with its Franciscan background, and the cathedral community of the Kilkenny colony.

The other manuscript which exhibits a correspondence with the Red Book is British Museum MS. Cotton Titus A. xx. Here stanzas 1, 4, 5, 6, and 8 of No. 52 occur as lines 97-100, 101-108, and 113-120 of the long poem given the title 'De Maria Virgine' by its only editor, Thomas Wright.[3] The stanzas which occur in both of these English manuscripts are Nos. 1, 4, 6, 8 of the Red Book poem. Stanza 8, which begins the second of the two poems in the Bibliothèque Nationale manuscript, is found in the Cotton manuscript as part of 'De Maria Virgine'. The second, fourth, fifth, sixth and seventh stanzas of the second Paris poem, not paralleled in the Red Book, are found in 'De Maria Virgine' as lines 121-136. This material has obviously been in general circulation, with consequent omissions and interpolations.

Nos. 48 and 51 in the Red Book have also been taken from 'De Maria Virgine' or a common source. Of No. 48 the first and last stanzas also appear as lines 45-48 and 69-72 of the long poem; of No. 51 the first five stanzas occur, not consecutively but as lines 181-188, 201-208, and 213-216.

---

1. Compare the "Sermon on the Body of the Lord", probably preached at Orvieto in 1264, in M.C. D'Arcy, ed., Selected Writings of St. Thomas Aquinas (N.Y., 1950), p.27: "O living Bread, begotten in heaven, barmed in the womb of the Virgin, baked in the furnace of the Cross, brought forth to the altar under the disguise of the wafer."
2. Poems of John of Hoveden, Surtees Society Publications, CLIV (London, 1939), xlviii, and personal communication.
3. The Latin Poems Attributed to Walter Mapes, Camden Society, No. XVI (London, 1841), 191-207.

It is only among the first forty-seven pieces that we find the songs which have prefixed to them the often-cited fragments of English and French. Some comment on these fragments may now be given in the order of their first appearance.

One of them is used three times, with Nos. 8, 19 and 28.   With No. 19 it reads:

>   Haue mercie on me, frere,
>   Barfote that ygo.

With Nos. 8 and 28 only the first line is given.   Brown and Robbins's <u>Index of Middle English Verse</u> calls this 'a fragmentary refrain of a popular song'.[1] But all three of the Latin pieces which are metrically modelled on it have the same verse-form, a four-line cross-rhymed stanza without refrain or burden, so that we must assume that the two English lines are not a refrain but the beginning of a stanza.   The first two stanzas of No. 28, an Easter song, will show what the rhythm of the Middle English piece must have been:

>   Maria, noli flere
>   Sepulcra Domini;
>   Surexit enim vere
>   Sepultus ab heri.
>
>   Sepulcra patuere
>   Testantur angeli;
>   Ad latus intuere
>   Quem vocas raboni.

The same two rhymes are used throughout the six stanzas, and the rhyme-sound in the odd lines of the Latin is the same as in the first line of the English text: 'flere-frere'.   We can be quite certain that the two English lines are the beginning of the first stanza of an otherwise unknown English song in four-line cross-rhymed stanzas without a burden.

The fragment prefixed to No. 11 is the most interesting of all, since it demonstrates the identity of one of the songs current among the young clergy of Kilkenny and the lyrics, often, with no good reason, called 'minstrel' songs, of Bodleian Library MS. Rawlinson D. 913.   These songs are found on a vagrant half-leaf of parchment and constitute almost all that is preserved of early fourteenth-century English secular lyric.   Not all of them are complete; some are mere jottings.   The writer or compiler of the little strip of poetry is unknown, and the only clue to its provenance is a mention in one song of Coggeshall, Essex, in connection with a man's

---

1.   (N.Y., 1943), No. 1123.

penniless condition. Coggeshall had a Cistercian monastery which held an
annual fair of regional, though hardly of national, fame, so that we can
safely believe that the songs come from eastern England. It was more
probably a monk or novice who wrote them down than anyone who may
properly be called a minstrel, that is a layman playing an instrument pro-
fessionally. Of these songs in the Rawlinson scrap the finest is 'The Maid
of the Moor'; indeed, it is one of the most haunting lyrics of all the Middle
Ages.[1] It is in a rondel verse-form which is not found elsewhere in Middle
English, nor does it occur, to my knowledge, in any other medieval Latin
verse.[2]

    In the margin at the head of No. 11 is a stain which somewhat ob-
scures the writing underneath. The editors of the Historical Manuscripts
Commission report, who were doubtless tired and cold and anxious to get
back to England, merely called the words 'indecipherable'. But a closer
inspection yields a clear reading of 'mayde yn the moore lay'. The odds
against any one song's appearing thus in these two manuscripts are obviously
enormous, but there the correspondence is. It can be seen at once how
the Latin 'not only follows the line and stanza pattern of the English rondel,
but preserves much of its characteristic lilt'.[3] If only we knew the tune
we should have no trouble at all in making it serve for both. The first
stanzas of the two pieces may be set side by side to show the likeness:

        Maiden in the mor lay,   Peperit virgo,
          In the mor lay,   Virgo regia,
        Seuenyst fulle,   Mater orphanorum,
        Seuenyst fulle;   Mater orphanorum;
        Maiden in the mor lay,   Peperit virgo,
          In the mor lay,   Virgo regia,
        Seuenistes fulle,   Mater orphanorum,
       [Seuenistes fulle]   Mater orphanorum,
        Ant a day.   Plena gracia.

---

1.   A convenient text is in R.H. Robbins, ed., Secular Lyrics of the
        XIVth and XVth Centuries, 2nd ed. (Oxford, 1955), p.12.
2.   The user of Brown and Robbins's Index of Middle English Verse may
        need to be warned against the designation of this poem as a fragment
        of a carol. It is entered by the first line of its second stanza as No.
        3891 with a cross-reference. Robbins's Secular Lyrics does not
        repeat the mistake, and the Supplement to the Index by Robbins and
        Cutler deletes the entry (Lexington, Kentucky, 1965).
3.   Richard L. Greene, "'The Maid of the Moor' in the Red Book of
        Ossory," Speculum, XXVII (1952), 504-506.

The inclusion of 'The Maid of the Moor' among the cantilenae teatrales, turpes, et seculares which would pollute sanctified throats prevents acceptance of the truly amazing attempt of Professor D.W. Robertson (who was followed by R.J. Schoeck) to interpret the song as a religious lyric filled with Christian symbolism.[1] Professor Robertson's exegesis, for which he tells us, Professor Bernard F. Huppé shares responsibility, is a little classic of misplaced ingenuity, written without knowledge of the marginal entry. The quoted first line and the verse-form, highly unusual if not unique, and shared by the English and the Latin, would seem to have forbidden any continued entertainment of the notion that the maiden is herself the Virgin and that 'her bower consisted of the roses of martyrdom or charity and the lilies of purity'. Professor E. Talbot Donaldson has rejected Robertson's reading on other grounds than those of the marginal note, and most of the critics who have commented on the poem in recent years have regarded it as a secular piece.[2]

But some readers who cherish the curious thesis that all popular as well as learned medieval poetry must have a basis in formal theology have been determined to explain away the highly inconvenient exception which the lovely little song presents. (One can only wonder how they visualize the consciousness of the vast uneducated majority, especially that of its younger generation.) Two conspicuous attempts have recently been made. One, by Professor Edmund Reiss, offers an extensive and detailed 'explication', of which the scattered parts are chiefly unified by the a priori assumption that there must be religious symbolism in the verses.[3] A sample of its quality can be seen in its suggestion that there is numerical symbolism - that the number of 'completeness or totality, and more specifically of the seven ages of the world' determines the number of lines in each stanza. Unfortunately, the number of lines in each stanza, as shown by the rhymes and the Latin counterpart, is nine. Then the number of the stanzas, four, when multiplied by seven gives the significant product of twenty-eight, which 'was viewed in neo-Pythagorean thought as a perfect number'. But it is by no means certain that the English song as we have it is complete - more stanzas to follow are strongly suggested, and it occurs, not as Reiss states, in 'a volume of secular verse', but on a single leaf of mostly fragmentary and patently popular songs.

---

1. Robertson, "Historical Criticism," English Institute Essays, 1950, ed. A.S. Downer (N.Y., 1951); Schoeck, TLS, June 8, 1951, p.357. Speculum, XXVII (1952), 115.
2. "Patristic Exegesis: the Opposition," Critical Approaches to Medieval Literature: Selected Papers from the English Institute 1958-59, ed. Dorothy Bethurum (N.Y., 1960), pp. 23-24.
3. The Art of the Middle English Lyric: Essays in Criticism (Athens, Georgia, 1972), pp.98-106.

The other attempt to force the Maid of the Moor into the patristic straitjacket is even more ambitious. Joseph Harris has published twenty-nine pages of argument designed to show that the song is not only a religious one but also one derived from a ballad, widespread in continental Europe, though not in England, about Mary Magdalene.[1] He also strongly suggests that the central figure of the song is the Virgin as well. Alas, in spite of the 'miraculous change' which he mentions in his final sentence, if there was one thing which the Magdalene was not, it was a maiden. In an attempt to support his view Harris hints, apparently without having seen the Red Book itself, that the present editor's reading of the crucial marginal note may not be correct. He also offers a challenge to the interpretation here given to the manuscript section's colophon. He claims that it does not say that the Latin songs are in any way sacred parodies or based on vernacular songs and that 'the fragments of vernacular song are not in any sense the models of the Latin poems'. It is true that the Latin poems are not parodies in the way of adapting but retaining in part the verbal originals, but no claim of that kind has been made by the present editor. Acquaintance with the texts of all the songs, which Harris does not appear to have, should quickly dispel this fallacious attempt to disprove what he calls 'the error'. It is also quite true that the colophon urges the clerks of Kilkenny to find tunes for the songs, and many are left for the clerks themselves to set airs to, but there were doubtless many popular tunes in circulation which would fit more than one of the songs, and the colophon in no way implies, as Harris would have it do, that the Latin verses are based on some other metrical patterns. No lengthy refutation is needed - an acquaintance with the ways of later broadside tunes would suffice. One other point about the article must be made: a ballad is a narrative by definition, and the lyric of the Maid of the Moor does not possess the similarity to ballad style which is alleged. Rarely has so delicate a butterfly been broken upon so ponderous a wheel.

Luckily, if another piece of objective evidence for the secular and popular character of the song were needed, it is brilliantly supplied by Professor Siegfried Wenzel's discovery of some lines quoted in a fourteenth-century Latin sermon in Worcester Cathedral Library MS. F. 126.[2] The quotation occurs in an indisputably secular context from Ovid and Boethius concerning the classical Golden Age. The crucial passage is "'Et quis potus? Respondltur in quodam cantico, viz. karole 'þe mayde be wode lay,' nota in margine: 'þe cold water of þe well spryng.'" The reference

---

1. "'Maiden in the Mor Lay' and the Medieval Magdalen Tradition," The Journal of Medieval and Renaissance Studies, I (1971), 59-87. Harris provides a useful bibliographical note on the discussions of the lyric (n. 8).
2. "The Moor Maiden - A Contemporary View," Speculum, XLIX (1974), 69-74.

to this English song cannot be doubted, though there is here a wood (better for violets than a moor!). Its being called 'karole' need not trouble us, for while it has not the burden-and-stanza form of the English carol usually so called, it is in another form derived from the dance of the carole - a rondel. Professor Wenzel has briefly and clearly reinforced the conclusion that the English poem 'was a secular dance-song dealing with a figure from medieval folklore'.

To No. 17 is prefixed the longest of all the bits of English verse, five lines, rhymed aabba:

   Alas, how sholdy synge?
   Yloren is my playinge:
   How sholdy with that olde man
   To leuen and let my lemman,
   Swettist of al thinge?

The listing of this piece in Brown and Robbins's Index of Middle English Verse under its third line (as No. 1265, cross-indexed to its first line), results from an attempt to interpret it as 'A fragment of a love song, reconstructed as the first English carol - one quatrain and burden'. This view a consideration of the Latin song which follows it will not permit. The Latin piece, a plea to the Virgin to lighten the sinner's load of guilt, is without burden or refrain, not at all in the carol-form, and it shows us at once that what we have is a complete stanza of an English song in this five-line verse-form which is unusual in either English or Latin:

   Succurre, mater Christi,
   Menti mee tristi,
   Pondere peccati quo deprimitur
   Prorsus ad yma semper labitur
   Sine defensore.

Dr. Robbins repeated this interpretation on p.xxxvi in his Secular Lyrics of the XIVth and XVth Centuries but has since abandoned it. Not only the form of the Latin song, but the marking of the stanza with the usual stanza-sign in the manuscript shows that we must look elsewhere for 'the first English carol'.

We can, however, see clearly that this English song-stanza is the beginning of a chanson de mal mariée, one of the most frequent of subject-matter genres in late medieval French, but a rarity in English. In spite of a lack of lyric texts, we can tell from such a narrative work as Chaucer's Merchant's Tale what the uncourtly fourteenth-century English muse thought of the forced marriage of young and fresh girls to senile husbands. Some of us would be willing to exchange an equal number of lines from the Merchant's

Tale for the rest of this song which appears to have been liked only too well by the young vicars of St. Canice's. It would probably turn out to be something like the typical maumariée of which Rolland records several variants, one from the eighteenth century going thus:

(Long refrain omitted)

>Mon père aussi m'a marié
>A un viellard il m'a donné,
>Il n'a ny maille ny denier
>Qu'un seul bâton de vert pommier
>De quoi, il m'en bat les côtez
>S'il me bat cor, j m'en iray
>Avec ces gentils écoliers;
>Ils m'apprendrai le jeu d'aimer,
>Le jeu de cartes, le jeu de dez. [1]

One line of the long refrain, like the Kilkenny fragment, begins 'Hélas!' and goes on: 'mon Dieu est-ce qu'il me faut?' Or the rest of our piece might well be a song such as one recorded from the fifteenth century which begins:

>Si je suis trouvée
>Avecques mon amy,
>En doy je estre blasmée
>Pour parler à luy?

>Mon pere et ma mere   ,sy m'ont mariée
>A un vieil bon homme   . . . .
>Maudit soit le jour   qu'oncques je le vy!
>Hellas! mes amours   ne sont pas ycy. [2]

Another of the Middle English song-beginnings is used twice, written as a single line before a song on the Resurrection (No. 22) and as a couplet before a Nativity song (No. 34). The two lines are:

>'Do, do,' nyghtyngale syng(es) wel (ful) mury(e),
>'Shal Y neure for thyn loue lenger karie (kary).'

---

1. Rondes à danser, reprinted in E. Rolland, ed., Recueil de chansons populaires (Paris, 1883), I, 79. Compare, e.g., "La Maumariée," in Julien Tiersot, ed., Chansons populaires des Alpes françaises: Savoie et Dauphiné (Grenoble and Montiers, 1903), p.309, and following pieces.
2. Gaston Paris, ed., Chansons du XVe siècle, Société des Anciens Textes Français (Paris, 1875), No. V, p.51.

Interestingly, one of these Latin pieces is in stanzas only, while the other (No. 34) has a burden in form identical with the stanza, as is fairly common in medieval song. Both Latin pieces show the long pause or rest which must be inserted after the third measure, the presence of which we should hardly suspect from seeing the English alone. In the Latin song with the burden this pause is marked by internal rhyme:

> Regem adoremus
> > Superne curie;
> Matri iubilemus,
> > Regine glorie.
>
> Virgo pura carens
> > Lapis rubigine,
> Natum nobis parens
> > Deum in homine.
> > > (etc.)

In the other song (No. 22) the internal rhyme is occasional, as in some of the earlier hymns of the Middle Ages, and the metrical unit is obviously thought of as a stanza of two long lines:

> Dies ista gaudii, die leticie:
> De morte resurexit Christus hodie.
> > (etc.)

The Latin keeps the rhyme in -e throughout and uses as rhyme-words the following, doubtless suggested by the English myrie and karie: funer, viuere, credere, uulnere, carcere, scelere, munere.

Now what does the English couplet mean ? To understand it we must look outside of Middle English verse, abounding in nightingales though it is, and observe those ubiquitous birds in French song, both traditional and courtly. The bird here is the nightingale who has been the trusted messenger of lovers, who has carried letters and delivered tender messages by word of beak. Moreover, he seems to be a representative of the type which we may call the disillusioned or rebellious nightingale, found, for example, in a ronde à danser recorded by Ballard in 1724 in a number of variants:

> Rossignolet sauvage,
> Rossignolet chermant
> > Veudris-tu bien
> Me portér ine lettre
> > A moun' amant
> Tieu-là que mon tieur aime.

> Rossignol prend la lettre
> Chez la belle y s'en va
> Ah! dormé-vous,
> Sommeillé-vous la belle
> Pensé-vous ben
> A tieu-là qui ve z'aime   [1]
>
> (etc.)

Or it might have ended like another <u>ronde à danser</u> also recorded by Ballard and still very much alive in France. In this the bird, encountered as usual in a garden

> me disoit en son latin,
> 'Fille, croyez-moi, n'aymez point
> Car les garçons ne valent rien
> Et les hommes encore moins.'   [2]

Apparently the Kilkenny clerks knew a song which began with somewhat similar speech by a bird:

> 'Do, do,' the nightingale sings merrily indeed;
> 'I shall never more report or take messages for
>   your love.'

The two lines prefixed to No. 30 have many parallels in English traditional song:

> Gayneth me no garlond of greene,
> Bot hit ben of wythoues ywroght.

That is: 'No green garland is suitable for me unless it is made of willow branches'. It is obvious that this is a bit of one of the many songs using the willow as the badge of the forsaken lover of either sex. [3] But the structure of its Latin counterpart shows that we must not call it, as Brown and Robbins's <u>Index</u> does, 'a fragmentary refrain of a forsaken maiden's lament'. [4] It could be the complaint of a lovelorn clerk, and the Latin song has neither burden nor refrain. It is a moral poem against trust in worldly benefits:

1. Rolland, <u>op</u>. <u>cit</u>., I, 44.
2. Ibid., I, 45.
3. On the tradition of the willow in English songs of the lovelorn see Frederick W. Sternfeld, "Shakespeare's Use of Popular Song," <u>Elizabethan and Jacobean Studies Presented to Frank Percy Wilson</u> (Oxford, 1959), pp.154-162.
4. No. 891.

xvi

> Verum est quod legi satis plene
> Codice sacro volumine:
> Felix est qui moritur hic bene,
> Celitus pro Christi nomine.
>
> (etc.)

The writer of the Latin seems to have had not merely the tune but the English words in his mind as he wrote, for throughout all five stanzas the odd lines have rhyme-words in -ene, like the 'greene' of the vernacular song. With the rather slow and solemn metrical movement of the Latin to guide us we can read understandingly the English lines, which by themselves would hardly suggest to us the right rhythm for the lost tune: five accents to the line. We may wish that it were as easy to reconstruct the melody.

Shortest of all the English phrases is that prefixed to No. 24:

> Haue god day, my lemmon. &c.

As this is one measure short of the line of Latin which begins the poem we can feel safe in assuming that a word such a 'dere' or 'swete' must have followed 'lemmon'. The Latin begins with the burden:

> Resurgenti cum gloria
> Gaudeat Ecclesia,
> Digne cantans alleluya.

The stanzas have four lines, and the rhyme in -a is kept throughout. In the fashion frequent in French dance-song forms but unusual in English, the first line of the external burden is used as an internal refrain in each stanza:

> Rumpenti mortis vincula,
> Resurgenti cum gloria,
> Pede calcanti tartara
> Vite reddenti premia.
>
> (etc.)

If we had only No. 24 to go on, we should have to remain uncertain whether the brief lover's greeting is the beginning of a burden or of a stanza. But the verse-form is exactly the same as that of No. 23, next before, and to No. 23 is prefixed a Latin line as indication of tune: 'En Christi fit memoria'. That is the first line of No. 7, which is in the same metre and likewise rhymed in -a throughout. From what we know of the scribe's procedure we can interpret the direction as meaning: 'Sing No.23 to the same tune that you use for No. 7'. Since the Latin <u>incipit</u> used for this purpose is the first line of a burden, we can be all but positive that 'Have

xvii

god day, my lemmon' is the incomplete first line of the burden of the lost English song, a carol.

The last of the English fragments is the least clear of all in its relation to the Latin which follows it, but it offers a highly interesting occurrence of an obscure word. It is written in one line but was apparently sung as two:

  Hey, how, the cheualdoures wokes al nyght.

The Nativity song associated with it (No. 41) has a burden made up of two four-accent lines, each repeated once, and a stanza of the most frequent type of all, of three lines rhymed and a <u>cauda</u>:

   En parit virgo regia,
   En parit virgo regia,
   Maria plena gracia,
   Maria plena gracia.

  In vtero sanctificata,
  Ab angelo dum nunciata,
  Spiritu Sancto inpregnata,
   Deum parit in homine.

    (etc.)

It seems certain that we have in the English a burden and not a stanza-beginning because of the exclamatory 'Hey, how!' The burden of an English carol about marital strife goes:

  Hey, howe! sely men,
  God help you.[1]

This, as the song writers handle metre, is in the same metre as the Red Book line and could be sung to the same air. Recalling the case of 'The Maid of the Moor', where the fuller text in the Rawlinson manuscript shows repetition corresponding, except for one line, to that of the matching Latin song, we suspect the same intent here. The most likely guess is that the English is a burden which would be sung like this:

  Hey, how! the chevaldoures,
  Hey, how! the chevaldoures
   Wokes al nyght,
   Wokes al nyght.

---

1. Greene, <u>The Early English Carols</u>, No. 409.

But what are these chevaldoures ? Frances A. Foster has discussed the word at length because of its importance for the dating of the Fasciculus Morum, but does not notice the Red Book song. [1] At about 1317 it means gentlemen cattle-raiders on the Border. Later on it has generally been glossed as 'vagabonds' or 'wasters': in the fifteenth-century English-Latin glossary Promptorium Parvulorum we find 'Discussor, vagabundus', and a quotation from the Catholicon of 'vagus, vagulus'. [2] The new Middle English Dictionary, unfortunately, does not go as far as Miss Foster's account. I believe that in this English song the word has a more specialized meaning, the clues to which come from two English Wycliffite tracts found in their manuscript near to another tract condemning singing and dancing, especially at Christmas time. One passage attacks curates who feast their patrons and 'oþere getteris of countre & ydel schaueldouris', and the other condemns the giving of costly clothes to 'riche men, & mynstralis or shaualdours for worldly name'. [3] The coupling of the word with 'mynstralis' is arresting. Another illuminating passage, much better known, occurs in William Dunbar's Remonstrance to the King, that is, to James IV of Scotland. The poem is one of Dunbar's numerous appeals to his monarch for more reward and favour. His effect, as often elsewhere, depends on a cumulative catalogue, so that the beginning of the poem must be quoted at some length:

> Schir, ye have mony servitouris
> And officiaris of dyvers curis;
> Kirkmen, courtmen, and craftismen fyne,
> Doctouris in jure and medicyne,
> Divinouris, rethoris, and philosophouris,
> Men of armes and vailyeand knychtis,
> And mony uther gudlie wichtis;
> Musicianis, menstralis, and mirrie singaris,
> Chevalouris, cawandaris, and flingaris,
> Cunyouris, carvouris, and carpentaris,
> Beildaris of barkis and ballingaris,
> Masounis lyand upon the land,
> And schipwrichtis hewand upone the strand,
> Glasing wrichtis, goldsmythis, and lapidaris,
> Pryntouris, payntouris, and potingaris;
> And all of thair craft cunning
> And all at anis lawboring,

---

1. "Some English Words from the 'Fasciculus Morum'", Essays and Studies in Honor of Carleton Brown (N.Y., 1940), pp. 155-156.
2. Ed. A.L. Mayhew, E.E.T.S., Extra Series, No. CII (1908), col. 394. Compare Lydgate, Assembly of Gods, l. 675, E.E.T.S., Extra Series, No. LXIX, p.21.
3. F.D. Matthew, ed., The English Works of Wyclif Hitherto Unprinted, E.E.T.S., Original Series, No. 74 (1880), p.249 (from "Why Poor Priests Have No Benefice") and p. 210 (from "How Satan and His Children", etc.).

>   Quhilk pleisand ar and honorable
>   And to your hienes profitable. [1]

    This is a carefully classified as well as alliterated list, and lest we fail to see what they all have in common, Dunbar spells it out for us: they are all skilled artists or craftsmen who know their business and work hard at it. Moreover, the subdivisions of the list are logical; if Dunbar had meant by <u>chevalouris</u> any kind of men at arms, even vagabond free-lances, he would have put them with the other knights.   Indeed, he goes on to list the other kinds of retainers, the unworthy and objectionable folk who pretend to serve the King while really serving only themselves and the cause of disorder and strife:

>   Bot ye sa gracious ar and meik
>   That on your hienes follows eik
>   Ane uthir sort, more miserabill,
>   Thocht thai be nocht sa profitable:
>   Fenyeouris, fleichouris, and flatteraris,
>   Cryaris, craikaris, and clatteraris,
>
>   . . .
>
>   Thrimlaris and thristaris as thay war woid,
>   Kokenis, and kennis na man of gude,
>   Schulderaris and schowaris that hes no schame,
>   And to no cunning than can clame,
>   And can non uthir craft nor curis
>   Bot to mak thrang, schir, in your duris. [2]

    If 'chevalours' in Dunbar's vocabulary were a synonym for any kind of sinister outlaw or useless loafer, it would have appeared in the second list and not in the first. Unfortunately the latest editor of the poem gives us no help at all, omitting the word from both notes and glossary. 'Flingaris' are dancers clearly enough, but the other noun in the critical line is 'cawandaris', and all that the same editor can do with that is to list it in the glossary with the notation 'obscure'. But the conclusion seems inescapable that 'chevaldoures' bore in both fourteenth- and fifteenth-century English the meaning of 'professional entertainers', perhaps the mummers who mixed music, posture, and acting, the <u>lusores</u> who are rewarded in royal and monastic household accounts along with minstrels and singers.   It is possible that 'chevaldoures' indicates in the Red Book

1.   Poems, ed. James Kinsley, Clarendon Medieval and Tudor Series (Oxford, 1958), 11, 1-20, pp. 88-89.
2.   II. 35-40, 47-52.

wandering musicians not attached to any nobleman's retinue or to any civic
or ecclesiastical corporation. Thus understood, it gives our song-line a
sense which has not before this been recognised in it. 'Wokes' has surely
the specialized meaning of 'kept a wake', i.e., an all-night celebration
on the eve of a saint's day, just the kind of solatium that the Bishop, like
many another medieval churchman, was much worried about and at which
the men of music would be sure to turn up. We can then render the fragment thus: 'Hey, how! The wandering musicians kept the wake going all
night'.

Along with these English song-beginnings there appear two in French,
written in the same way and obviously intended to indicate songs whose
tunes and verse-forms were to be used for the Latin pieces following them.
Both are single couplets, and both express, with the succinctness and direct-
ness that are marks of French traditional song from the Middle Ages to the
present, the pain of love that has not prospered. Neither one has turned
up in the course of a search through many hundreds of French lyrics of many
centuries. But both ring perfectly true when one returns to them after a
course of reading in the many songs of similar themes and spirit.

The first couplet is prefixed to a Nativity song, No. 18:

   Harrow! leo su trahy
   Par fol amour de mal amy.

It appears to be the beginning of some one of the countless songs in which
a betrayed and abandoned girl is the speaker. No suggestion of this theme
can be found in the Latin verses, which are in the carol-form with the first
line of the burden repeated as an internal refrain-line, the second of each
stanza. The French couplet appears to have been a burden and not the
opening of the first stanza:

   Jhesu, lux vera seculi,
   Tui te laudant seruuli.
   Gaudent videntes angeli,
   Jhesu, lux vera seculi;
   Pandunt melos preconii
   Ob diem natale tui.

    (etc.)

The rhyme-sound of -i is taken over from the vernacular lines and is used
throughout.

The other French couplet is prefixed to No. 40, a poem addressed to Mary and celebrating the Presentation in the Temple. It is also a lament beginning with an exclamation:

> Heu, alas, par amour,
> Qy moy myst en taunt dolour.

The song which follows has no burden, but uses the four-line stanza rhymed aaab with the b's of all the stanzas rhyming together which is frequent in the medieval lyric of various languages. If, as seems most likely, we have in the French simply the first two lines of such a stanza, the Latin text can without difficulty be seen as singable to the same music, with the substitution of a two-syllable rhyme-word for the one long syllable and the following pause or rest which the French uses. Here, as in some other pieces, the Latin text shows a freedom from exact correspondence in the syllables as against the accents of different stanzas which is rather like the syllabic freedom in vernacular song and which is fully in keeping with the use of vernacular rather than Latin models. Stanza 5 may illustrate:

> Impuritatem tu que nescis,
> Puris tamen data cum sis,
> Purificari quomodo scis,
> Immunis ab exteris.

In fact, Richard de Ledrede seems to have proceeded much as Robert Burns described himself as doing four centuries later, to have got the tune running in his head and then to have proceeded by ear rather than by strict count of syllables. The relationship between the English and the Latin seems to have been somewhat like that between Scots and English as Burns himself explains it: 'There is a certain irregularity in the old Scotch Songs, a redundancy of syllables with respect to that exactness of Accent & measure that the English poetry requires, but which glides in most melodiously with the respective tunes to which they are set.'[1] And if Richard lacks the genius of Burns, he has yet little to be ashamed of in his work of producing Latin lyrics which go trippingly on the tongue.

---

1. First Common-place Book, September 1785, in Works, ed. W.S. Douglas (Edinburgh, 1895), IV, 93. Compare Friedrich Gennrich, Musikwissenschaft und romanische Philologie (Halle a. S., 1918), p.4: "Es ist allgemein bekannt, dass es in der Liedliteratur sog. Contrafakta, d.h. Lieder gibt, die in bewussten Anlehnung an irgend ein berühmtes oder bekanntes Vorbild nachgebildet wurden. Man geht wohl nicht irre, wenn man die Melodie des Vorbildes als Hauptfaktor für das Entstehen eines Contrafaktums ansieht; weicht doch der Gedankenheit des Vorbilden von dem des Contrafaktums gewöhnlich sehr stark ab. Besonders geistliche Lieder pflegen sich

. . . . .

While it is obvious that a great many of the Middle English religious
carols and other lyrics, like the Gude and Godlie Ballatis of later Scots,
result from the same kind of religious parody and imitation of secular song
that we find in the Red Book, there are no other English records of the process
that are so circumstantial and that offer us so many vernacular tags for
identification.[1] But the presence in the Red Book of the French fragments
along with the English is a sign of what we should assume even without it:
the trilingual habits of the young clerks. They have a counterpart in the
Oxfordshire scholar, Wymundus London, who in Gonville and Caius College,
Cambridge, MS. 383 has recorded for us some of the finest secular carols in
English and has also included a carol to St. Catherine in French.[2] The
whole exercise-book shows him to have the expected knowledge of Latin as
well.

A few of the examples from the continent of Europe of the use of
vernacular songs to give form and tune to religious pieces in Latin will
illuminate by analogy the procedure followed by the Bishop of Ossory.

An early set of contrafacta, to borrow the musicologists' useful term,
is that left us by Adam de la Bassée, Canon of the church of St. Peter at
Lille, who died in 1286. Adam wrote an adaptation, or rather a slavish
imitation, of the famous Anticlaudianus of Alain de l'Isle, a work which he
performed to distract himself from his bodily pains when he was ill and
suffering. That is about all that we know of his biography.[3] At intervals
he inserted original Latin lyrics on religious and moral themes, some using

---

        an weltliche, bekannte Lieder anzulehnen, - eine Tatsache, die sich
        nicht nur auf das Mittelalter in Frankreich allein beschränkt, sondern
        bis auf den heutigen Tag in noch vielen anderen Ländern sich
        nachweisen lässt, --" Gennrich refers to the songs of Adam de la
        Bassée as examples. See also Hans Spanke, 'Das öftere Auftreten
        von Strophenformen und Melodien in der altfranzösischer Lyrik,"
        Zeitschrift für französische Sprache und Litteratur, LI (1928), 84, 91-93.
1.   Examples in The Early English Carols include: No. 261, 'A song vpon
        (now must I syng &c.)" and No. 93, "A song in the tvne of/and I were
        a mayd &c."
2.   Greene, The Early English Carols, pp. xxvi-xxvii.
3.   See Paul Bayart, ed., Ludus Adae de Basseia Canonici Insulensis
        Super Anticlaudianus (Tourcoing, 1930), pp. xiii-xv. This edition
        gives photographic reproductions and modern transcriptions of the
        songs, thirty-eight in all. Ten of them have indications of the airs
        of vernacular songs, eleven have similar references to Latin hymns,
        sequences, alleluias, or responses, and the rest have music ostensibly
        composed by Adam himself.

the verse-forms of familiar Latin liturgical pieces, such as Veni creator spiritus and the famous prose Laetabundus, but others modelled on vernacular songs which included both chansons by identified trouvères and, what does not appear at all at Kilkenny, one motet or polyphonic piece. For example, Adam writes an eight-line, one-stanza reflection De Vanitate Mundi in the words of his rubric:

> Supra cantilenam quae incipit: Quant voi la flor parois for le. . .bet ke li dous tans dester se reclarcist. 1

What the flower and the sweet time of summer suggest to him is:

> O quam fallax est mundi gloria.

Another in the same form is in praise of St. Agnes, but its tune and stanza are those of Tant ai amors siervie longement. 2 The chanson of Raoul de Soissons which begins

> Quand voi la glaie meure et le rosier espanier

moves him to the praise of St. John the Baptist, whose day, to be sure, is Midsummer Day itself. 3

We should recognize another of Adam's models as a typical pastourelle even if he did not mark his composition: Super pastoralem, quae incipit: Lautrier estoie montes sor mon palefroi amblant. 4 But his theme is very different from that of the poem by Henri, Duc de Brabant, which he is following in tune and metre.   Quotation of one stanza will show how the Latin of the first two lines corresponds in rhythm to his vernacular model and also how successfully medieval Latin can be formed into stanzas even more complex than those of 'The Maid of the Moor' yet completely singable:

> Felix, qui humilium
>   Vere vitam sequitur,
> Vita namque talium
>   Gaudens exantabitur,
>   Sicut legitur;
> In contrarium
>   Fastus non assequitur

---

1.   Bayart, p. 54.
2.   Ibid., p. 76.
3.   Ibid., p. 85.
4.   Ibid., p. 129.

Caeli gaudium,
   Teritur, quatitur,
Solium
   Perdit, qui extollitur.

At least one of the songs which Adam used as models is a piece which was danced to, as we must suppose at least some of the Kilkenny songs to have been, for the Latin piece based on it, Nobilitas ornata, is marked: Cantilena de chorea, super illam quae incipit: 'Qui grieve ma cointise se iou l ai ce me sont amouretes c au cuer ai." [1]

A somewhat similar collection of Latin cantilenae, showing on the whole rather less metrical resourcefulness and rather more academic, not to say pedantic, flavour, is found in another manuscript of the late thirteenth century, formerly at Saint-Denis, but now in the Bibliothèque Nationale, numbered 15131. The texts of its twenty-seven songs may be found in the invaluable twentieth volume of Analecta Hymnica. They have been ascribed by Hauréau to a secular clerk who taught grammar at Saint-Denis. [2] They are obviously designed for the use of students and include three pieces in honour of Catherine, the patroness, and four in honour of Nicholas, the patron, of scholars. Some of them are in some variation of the carol-form with initial burden. Three of the songs have vernacular lines prefixed in the fashion of the Red Book. Quotation of two of these must suffice. A cantilena for All Saints' Day in seven-line stanzas bears the rubric: Detele heure vi labiante madame guene puis sanz li Contra in Latino: Sion concio etc. The burden of the Latin piece goes:

   Sion concio
   Ἀνὰ jubilet
   Cum tripudio

The nightingale is here, too, as well as at Kilkenny. One of the songs of St. Nicholas is headed:

   Joi te rossignol
   Chantez de sus i rain,
   Viar dinet namie
   De sus laure florie

   Contra in Latino: Sancti Nicolai etc.

The quoted French lines must have been the burden of a song in carol-form, for the burden of the Latin piece follows their metre:

1. See Paul Bayart, op.cit., p.147.
2. B. Hauréau, Notices et extraits de quelques manuscrits latins de la Bibliothèque Nationale (Paris, 1890), IV, 278.

Sancti Nicolai
vacemus titulis
Cum summa laetitia
Pangentes Alleluja.

That somewhat similar situations and similar remedies were to be found in medieval Germany is shown by a collection of Latin cantilenae forming part of the large and elaborate manuscript known as the Mosburg Gradual, University of Munich MS. 157. These songs differ from the work of Bishop Richard de Ledrede in that they are not accompanied by any note of association with identified secular and vernacular songs, but the long preface which introduces a set of Latin pieces shows so much of the same purpose as the Bishop's that it should be noticed. In it, John de Perchausen, Dean of the Church of Mosburg, tells how he has collected songs handed down in tradition within the church and has added to them some of his own composition, made when he was rector of the scholars. Part of his purpose is to prevent damage to the discipline of the choir at the time of the Nativity when the boy-bishop holds forth and 'the mirth of worldly songs' threatens to intrude with consequent laughter and ribaldry. It ends by recording John's hope that at the Nativity time 'praise and hymnic worship' might be shown to the Infant Saviour 'decently and reverently in these songs by the new little clerks, as if from the mouth of babes and sucklings, the indecency of the common sort being laid aside.'[1]

John has taken the trouble to mark with his name and to have the scribe rubricate those songs which he personally composed. They resemble the songs of the Red Book, with which they are exactly contemporary, in two major respects, their variety of metrical form and their use of the external burden of the type familiar in the English carol.

The most striking and interesting parallel of all to the Red Book of Ossory is found in another literally red book - the Liber Vermell of the great monastery of Montserrat, at present a centre of Catalan national feeling and in the late Middle Ages a most important place of pilgrimage.[2] The famous

---

1. The manuscript is briefly described and the songs somewhat imperfectly edited in Analecta Hymnica, XX, 22-23 and passim. For fuller discussion and textual improvements see Hans Spanke, "Das Mosburger Graduale," Zeitschrift für romanische Philologie, L. (1930), 582-595, and "Beziehungen zwischen Romanischer und mittellateinischer Lyrik," Abhandlungen der Gesellschaft der Wissenschaften zu Göttingen, Philologischhistorische Klasse, Dritte Folge, No. 18 (Berlin, 1936), 139.
2. Dom Gregorius Mª Suñol, "Els Cants dels Romeus (Segle XIVe)", Analecta Montserratensia, I (1918), 100-192. See also Spanke, "Beziehungen," pp. 127-30, and E. Louis Backman, Religious Dances in the Christian Church and in Popular Medicine, trans. E. Classen (London, 1952), p.96.

shrine of the Blessed Virgin high up on the spectacular saw-toothed mountain
was the reputed scene of many wonderful manifestations of her power, and a
small blackened statue was the focus of much reverent emotion. The
Benedictine monks, like those of other such places of crowded resort, had real
tasks of hospitality and discipline on their hands. Pilgrims who came on foot
entered the monastery in procession, and in addition to making their con-
fessions and attending the monks' services at the canonical hours, they watched
all night in a courtyard until time for early morning devotions. It was the
need to give these pilgrims an occupation which would be edifying and prevent
a natural tendency to beguile the time by singing worldly songs which led to
a duplication of the literary and musical expedient practised at Kilkenny.

The Liber Vermell of Montserrat, named, like that of Ossory, from its
red leather binding, is a large and handsome volume of about A.D. 1400,
which contains, like its Irish counterpart, a miscellany with a strong local
emphasis. Among its contents are an account of the miracles wrought by the
Blessed Virgin of Montserrat, a tract on confession, bulls of Boniface XI and
Benedict XIII, litanies to the Virgin, 'Geographica', 'Astronomica',
'Encyclopedia', a description of the churches of Rome, and tracts by Raymond
Lull. The most interesting part is a carefully made and handsomely written
collection of ten songs, in the Catalan vernacular and in Latin, with con-
siderable variety of musical and literary style. They are introduced by a
note similar to the memorandum in the Red Book of Ossory:

> Quia interdum peregrini quando vigilant in
> ecc[lesi]a beate marie de monte serrato, volunt cantare
> et tripudiare et etiam in platea de die. Et ibi non debeant
> nis[i] honestas ac devotas cantilenas cantare. Idcirco
> sup[er]ius et inferius alique sunt scripte. Et de hoc uti
> debent honeste et parce ne perturbent perseu[er]antes in
> or[ati]o[n]ibus et devotis contemplationibus in quibus omnes
> vigilantes insistere debent pariter et devote vaccare.[1]

Here it is definitely stated that the singing was accompanied by dancing, as
we may assume that it was at Kilkenny.

The ten songs may be briefly listed. Three of them provide
especially interesting comparisons with compositions in Bishop Richard de
Ledrede's series.

---

1.   Suñol, p. 106.

1.	O Virgo Splendida	Latin antiphon
2.	Stella splendens in monte	Latin dance-song in two parts
3.	Laudemus virginem	Latin 'rhythmus'
4.	Splendens captigera	Latin 'rhythmus'
5.	Los set gotxs recomptarem	Ballada for a round dance, in Catalan with responses in Latin
6.	Cuncti simul concanentes	Latin ballada for a round dance
7.	Polorum Regina	Latin song for a round dance
8.	Mariam matrem	Latin three-part song, with couplet burden
9.	Imperayuntz de la ciutat ioyosa	Catalan motet for two voices singing different words
10.	Ad mortem festinamus	Latin dansa, unison

The variety of this anthology makes it of great interest to the musicologist and the historian of Romance poetry. The most significant likeness to the cantilenae of Ossory is in the three songs which are in the burden-and-stanza form which we know from the English carol and in which so many of the Bishop's Latin songs are cast. If there should remain any doubt that the origin of this form is in the dance, the second of the Montserrat pieces should dispel it. The song is headed:

Sequitur alia cantilena o[mn]i dulcedine plena
eisde[m] dne nte ad tripudium rotundum

The burden shows at once that it is a song local to the monastery:

Stella splendens in monte   ut solis radium
miraculis serrato   exaudi populum

In the stanzas the pilgrims are made to sing of their own coming and of their different sorts and conditions:

1. Concurrunt universi   gaudentes populi
   divites et egeni   grandes et parvuli
   ipsum ingrediuntur   ut cernunt oculi
   et inde revertuntur   gracias repleti.

2. Principes et magnates   ex tirpe regia
    seculi potentates   obtenta venia
    peccaminu[m] p[ro]clama[n]t   tundentes pectora
    poplite flexo clamant   hic ave maria

    . . .

4. Rustici oratores   comites incliti
    advocati scultores   cuncti ligni fabri
    sartores et sutores   nec non lanifici
    artifices et omnes   gratulantur ibi. 1

There are seven stanzas in all, each followed by an explicit indication of the repetition of the burden. It will be noted that the metre is the same as that of Nos. 22 and 34 in the Ossory collection, the songs modelled on 'Do, do, nyghtyngale'.

The eighth song exhibits one of the characteristic features of a lyric form derived from the round dance, the <u>carole</u>, that is, the rhyming of the last word of the burden with the last word of each stanza as a kind of cue for the transition from solo part to chorus part. This rhyming persists here even though the music is for three voices throughout, just as it does in some polyphonic carols. The rhyme in this piece is on the adverbial ending -er:

>   Mariam matrem virginem attollite
>   Jesum [Christum] extollite concorditer

> Maria seculi asilum defende nos
> Jhesu tutum refugium exaudi nos
> Jam estis nos totaliter diffugium
> totum mundi confugium realiter

>   2. Jhesu supprema bonitas verissima
>   Maria dulcis pietas gratissima
>   Amplissima conformiter sit caritas
>   Ad nos quos pellit vanitas enormiter.

        . . .

>   5. Maria facta seculis salvatio
>   Jhesu dampnati hominis redemptio
>   Pugnare quam viriliter p[ro] famulis
>   percussis duris iaculis atrociter. 2

---

1. Suñol, pp. 122-123.
2. Ibid., p. 166.

The most striking of all the Montserrat songs is the last one, which brings a thoroughly macabre treatment of inevitable death into close association with the praise of the Virgin and the promise of merciful forgiveness in exactly the same way as several English carol manuscripts, which surprise the modern reader by offering a meditation on mortality with some variation of Timor mortis conturbat me as a burden right in the midst of festive and jovial pieces for the social celebration of Christmas. The humble singers of carols from oral tradition have brought the same juxtaposition down to modern times, e.g. with the use of 'Remember, O thou man' as a favourite Christmas carol. This last cantilena is to be sung in unison and danced to as well. It has the burden-and-stanza structure of the vernacular dance-song:

    Ad mortem festinam[u]s
    Peccare desistamus
    Peccare desistamus
  Scribere p[ro]posui
    De co[n]temptu mu[n]dano
  Vt degentes seculi
    No[n]mulce[n]tur i[n]vano.
  Iam est hora surge[re]
    A sompno mortis pravo
    A sompno mortis prava
    Iterum. Ad mortem festinamus [1]

There are nine stanzas in all. Its impressiveness for the reader of the manuscript itself is heightened by a line written in a different hand: 'O Mors, quam amara est memoria tua', and a realistic drawing of a skeleton in an open tomb, below which is written a kind of responsorial chant in seven lines, the first hemistich of each being 'Vil cadaver seras'. The similarity in feeling to the theme of the Dance of Death is obvious, but there is no reason to visualize any performance by the pilgrims more elaborate than their usual song-accompanied round dance or carole.

  In variety of metres used the Red Book of Ossory is not behind its counterparts on the Continent. Even after we have allowed for borrowing from other authors in some pieces, it is remarkable how many differing verse-forms Richard de Ledrede handled with apparently equal ease in this single garland of songs for practical devotional use. With the non-stanzaic form of the last poem excluded, there can be distinguished thirty-three different patterns of composition, two of two-line stanzas, one of three-line, twenty of four-line, two of five-line, three of six-line, two of seven-line, one each of eight- and nine-line, and one series of alternating two- and four-line stanzas. Of the fifty-nine some twenty-four conform to the pattern which we know as that of the English carol, using a burden sung initially

---

1. Sunol, p. 187.

and in unchanged form after every stanza.   This is greater metrical virtuosity
than is shown by most medieval hymn-writers working in the formal Latin
liturgical tradition.   Such variety and flexibility would lead us, even without the external evidence, to be sure of the operation of another influence,
that of the kind of song which we call 'popular' - perhaps 'informal' is a
better word - the song made by people at large in their own language and
from their own impulses.   And we are equally justified in reasoning back
from Bishop Richard's texts to the conclusion that Middle English song of the
secular public, that public to which, let it not be so often forgotten as it is,
every monk or friar or priest belonged before he became monk or friar or
priest, had many more metres and forms than the pathetically small preserved
remnant can show us.   The testimony of the Red Book of Ossory increases
our regret for the loss of what must have been thousands of light-hearted ditties,
some perhaps as beautiful as 'The Maid of the Moor', some certainly as rowdy
and rough as the song of the jovial drunkard which keeps it company on the
same worn and precious strip of parchment.

1

Of the Nativity

Cantilena de Natiuitate Domini

Verbum caro factum est
De virgine Maria.

Cuius nomen est Qui Est,
Verbum caro factum est,
Ab eterno natus est
De patris vsia.

    Verbum caro factum est
    De virgine Maria.

Cuius mater virgo est,
Verbum caro factum est,
Deus humanatus est,
Felix genologia.

    Verbum caro factum est
    De virgine Maria.

Saluator noster ipse est,
Verbum caro factum est,
Et iudex qui venturus est;
Non sit controuersia.

    Verbum caro factum est
    De virgine Maria.

Docet fides quod ita est,
Verbum caro factum est,
Redemptor mundi natus est;
Hec est salutis via.

Verbum caro f[a]c[tu]m est
De virgine Maria.

Cunctis creatis qui preest,
Verbum caro factum est,
Laus eius nobis adest;
Letemur mente pia.

Verbum caro factum est
De virgine Maria.

Amen.

Of the Nativity

Alia cantilena de eodem festo

Natus est de virgine
Rex glorie.

Sine viri semine
Natus est de virgine
Dei verbum
Caro factum
Hodie.

Natus est de virgine
Rex glorie.

Qui conceptus pridie
Natus est de virgine,
Incarnatus,
Humanatus
Hodie.

Natus est de virgine
Rex glorie.

Quem lex iubet colere
Natus est de virgine;
In presepi
Adoratur
Hodie.

Natus est de virgine
Rex glorie.

Felices excubie,
Natus est de virgine,
Angelorum
Et pastorum
Hodie.

Natus est de virgine
Rex glorie.

Voces pandunt glorie,
Natus est de virgine,
Deo laudem,
Mundo pacem,
Hodie.

Natus est de virgine
Rex glorie.

Pro tanto Dei munere,
Natus est de virgine,
Iocundemus
Et letemur
Hodie.

Natus est de virgine
Rex glorie.

3

Of the Nativity

De eodem festo

Vale, mater Christi,
Virgo regia,
In te mea spes.

Menti mee tristi,
Data venia,
Solamen tu es.

Vale, mater Christi,
Virgo regia,
In te mea spes.

Deum genuisti,
Dei filia,
Cuius mater es.

Vale, mater Christi,
[Virgo regia,
In te mea spes.]

Mortem sustulisti
Diuina gracia
Deum cum pareres.

Vale, mater Christi,
[Virgo regia,
In te mea spes.]

Vitam peperisti
Vite media
Mater cum fieres.

Vale, mater Christi,
[Virgo regia,
In te mea spes.]

Thronum possedisti
 Dei dextera,
Cum quo nunc resides.

Vale, mater Christi,
[Virgo regia,
In te mea spes.]

A te petunt celi
 Gloriam [ ]
Nobis vt impetres.

Vale, mater Christi,
Virgo regia,
In te mea spes.

Amen.

Burdens 3-6, II. 2, 3. Ms. &c.

4

Of the Nativity

De eodem festo

Nato Marie filio
 Congaudeat Ecclesia.

Verbo rerum principio,
Nato Marie filio,
Celi terreque Domino
 Collaudet mundi machina.

  Nato Marie filio
   Congaudeat Ecclesia.

Eterno Patris genito
Nato Marie filio,
Sed Spiritu Paraclito,
 De virgine puerpera.

  Nato Marie filio
   Congaudeat Ecclesia.

De summo celi solio,
Nato Marie filio,
Presentis vite stadio
 Se dedit nostri gracia.

  Nato Marie filio
   Congaudeat Eccl[es]ia.

Nascitur in stabulo,
Nato Marie filio,
Locatur in presepio
 Qui fabricauit omnia.

  Nato [Marie filio
   Congaudeat Ecclesia.]

Nutritur matris gremio,
Nato Marie filio,
Paruoque lactis pabulo,
 Celi pascens altilia.

  Nato [Marie filio
   Congaudeat Ecclesia.]

Pastorum contubernio,
Nato Marie filio,
Angelorum consorcio
  Cantatur alte gloria.

  Nato [Marie filio
    Congaudeat Ecclesia.]

Mundi pollens dominio,
Nato Marie filio,
Supernorum conuiuio
  Nos collocet in patria.

  Nato Marie filio
    Congaudeat Ecclesia.

    Amen.

Burdens 5-7. MS. Nato &c.

5

Of the Nativity

  Lingua, manu, opere,
  Exultemus et letemur
  Hodie.

Stude Christo psallere
Lingua, manu, opere,
  Nobis nato
  Nobis dato
    Munere.

Exultemus et letemur
  Hodie.

Venit nos redimere;
Lingua, manu, opere,
   Cedat fletus,
   Psallat cetus
     Hodie.
Exultemus (et letemur
     Hodie.]

Nos Deo coniungere,
Lingua, manu, opere,
   Noue legi
   Nato regi
     Glorie.
Exultemus (et letemur
     Hodie.]

Laus pro tanto munere,
Lingua, manu, opere,
   Sit sonora,
   Sit decora
     Culmine.
Exultemus (et letemur
     Hodie.]

Christo stude canere
Lingua, manu, opere;
   Pelle tussim,
   Tolle sitim
     Hodie.
Exultemus [et letemur
     Hodie.]

Tange ciphum propere,
Lingua, manu, opere,
   Funde potum,
   Bibe totum,
     Strenue.
Exultemus et letemur
     Hodie.

Nato laudem tribue
[Lingua, manu, opere,]
   Festo locum
   Lingue iocum
     Sobrie.
Exultemus [et letemur
   Hodie.]

Stanzas 2-5, 7, 11. 6, 7. MS. Exultemus &c.

6

Of the Nativity

Fons salutis nostre plene,
   Dei mater cum filio.

Grata Deo tue gene,
Fons salutis nostre plene,
Labe carens dire pene
   Matrum in puerperio.

   Fons salutis nostre plene,
     Dei mater cum filio.

Latrix pacis tam serene,
Fons salutis nostre plene,
Prolem foues, O quam bene,
   Tuo tenens gremio.

   Fons salutis nostre plene,
     Dei mater cum filio.

Tore matris hic terene,
Fons salutis nostre plene,
Lac mamillam ori tene
   Tam boni Patris filio.

Fons salutis nostre plene,
Dei mater cum filio.

Que Deum cibas tam amene,
Fons salutis nostre plene,
Ducas nos ad diem cene,
Perhenni sistens gaudio.

Fons salutis nostre plene,
Dei mater cum filio.

Amen.

7

To Christ

En Christi fit memoria,
Qua florent reflorent florida,
Da vera cordis gaudia.

Cuius forti potencia,
En Christi fit memoria,
Cuncta flectuntur genua,
Nutu fatentur subdita.

En Christi fit memoria,
Qua florent reflorent florida,
Da vera cordis gaudia.

Tu dela nostra facinora,
En Christi fit memoria,
Hostis pulsa nequicia,
Confirma cordis intima.

En Christi fit memoria,
Qua florent reflorent florida,
Da vera cordis gaudia.

Pacis propina pocula,
En Christi fit memoria,
Dissolue litis vincula,
Prebens eterna premia.

En Christi fit memoria,
Qua florent reflorent florida,
[Da vera cordis gaudia.]

After stanza 3.   am.
Burden 4, l. 3.   MS. &c.

8

Of the Epiphany

Haue mercy of me frere

Laus Christo reginato,
   Decus et gloria,
A magis adorato
   Honor in secula.

Thure deificato,
   Auro potencia,
Mirra mortificato
   Post vite tedia.

Herodes mala spirat
   Sua versucia,
Sed magos tu regiras
   Ad loca propria.

Tu aquas benedicis
> Baptismi gracia;
In vinum aquas vertis
> Mira potencia.

Qui reges ad te ducis
> Cum stella preuia,
Duc nos ad tue lucis
> Eterna premia.

> Amen.

9

Of the Nativity

Da, da nobis nunc;
Da colere solempnia festa;
Da paruuli promere gesta;
> Da, da nobis nunc.

Da, da nobis nunc;
Da matri laudis honorem;
Da paruulo cordis amorem;
> Da, da nobis nunc.

Da, da nobis nunc;
Da sic componere gestum,
Nil mestum, nil inhonestum;
> Da, da nobis nunc.

Da, da nobis nunc;
Da nunc corrigere mores,
Virtutum carpere flores;
> Da, da nobis nunc.

Da, da nobis nunc;
Da viuere vice iocunde,
Concedere satis et vnde;
    Da, da nobis nunc.

Da, da nobis nunc;
Da clero voluere libros;
Da populo tangere ciphos;
    Da, da nobis nunc.

Da, da nobis nunc;
Da prompte fundere potum;
Da sobrie bibere totum;
    Da, da nobis nunc.

Da, da nobis nunc;
Da paruulo psallere laudes;
Da procul pellere fraudes;
    Da, da nobis nunc.

Da, da nobis nunc;
Da mestis vim meritorum;
Da letis regna polorum;
    Da, [da] nobis nunc.

Da, da nobis nunc.

10

Of the Nativity

De radice virginis
    Flos vernans processit.

Ab alto diuini culminis,
De radice virginis,
Dei simul et hominis
    Natiuitas accessit.

    De radice virginis
        Flos vernans processit.

In ortu tanti mun[er]is,
De radice virginis,
Sedentibus in tenebris
    Lux vera lucessit.

    De radice virginis
        [Flos vernans processit.]

Huius ducatu germinis,
De radice virginis,
Peccatum Ade veteris
    Procul euanescit.

    De radice virginis
        [Flos vernans processit.]

Labe carens originis,
De radice virginis,
Vi Sancti Spiraminis
    Virgo pura pulcrescit.

    De radice virginis
        [Flos vernans processit.]

Data pace Christicolis,
De radice virginis,
Laus alta cum angelis
  In ore dulcessit.

De radice virginis
  [Flos vernans processit.]

Que vitam tulit morbidis,
De radice virginis,
Nobis deposcat miseris
  Que numquam marcessit.

De radice virginis
  Flos vernans processit.

    Amen.

Burdens 3-6, l. 2. MS. &c.

11

Of the Nativity

   Mayde y[n] the moore [l]ay.

Peperit virgo,
  Virgo regia,
Mater orphanorum,
Mater orphanorum;
Peperit virgo,
  Virgo regia,
Mater orphanorum,
Mater orphanorum,
  Plena gracis.

15

Prebuit honorem
   Vox angelica
Regi angelorum,
Regi angelorum;
[Prebuit honorem
   Vox angelica
Regi angelorum,
Regi angelorum,]
   Cantando gloria.

Puero feruntur
   Tria munera
Obsequio magorum,
Obsequio magorum;
[Puero feruntur
   Tria munera
Obsequio magorum,
Obsequio magorum,]
   Cum stella preuia.

Tribuat salutem
   Virgo celica,
Sola spes lapsorum,
Sola spes lapsorum;
[Tribuat salutem
   Virgo celica,
Sola spes lapsorum,
Sola spes lapsorum]
   In hac miseria.

Angelo docente
   Nati magnalia,
Vigilia pastor<u>um</u>,
Vigilia pastor<u>um</u>;
[Angelo docente
   Nati magnalia,
Vigilia pastorum,
Vigilia pastorum,]
   Laus <u>et</u> leticia.

V<u>i</u>rgo, p<u>re</u>ce pia
   P<u>er</u> tua mun<u>e</u>ra,
Regina sup<u>er</u>nor<u>um</u>,
Regina sup<u>er</u>nor<u>um</u>;
[Virgo, prece pia
   Per tua munera,
Regina supernorum,
Regina supernorum,]
   Duc nos ad supera.

      Amen.

Stanza 2, l. 9. Cantando MS. Cantantando.

12

Of the Nativity

Chr<u>i</u>sti p<u>a</u>rentele
   Laus D<u>o</u>mini;
Eiusq<u>ue</u> sequele
   Salus D<u>o</u>mini.

17

  Christi parentele
  Laus Domini;
  [Eiusque sequele
  Salus Domini.]

Matre manente
 Virgine,
Angelo docente
 Dei nomine.

  Christi parentele
  Laus Domini;
  [Eiusque sequele
  Salus Domini.]

Circumcidente
 Octaua die,
Iosep ministrante
 Tam strenue.

  Christi parentele
  Laus Domini;
  [Eiusque sequele
  Salus Domini.]

Maria fouente
 Tam sedule,
Puerum pascente
 Tam solicite.

  Christi parentele
  Laus Domini;
  [Eiusque sequele
  Salus Domini.]

Stella ducente
Ab oriente,
Magos adorante
Tr_i_no mun_e_re.

 Christi parentele
 Laus D_om_ini;
 Eiusq_ue_ sequele
 Salus D_om_ini.

Burdens 2-5, II. 3, 4. MS. &c.

13
Of the Epiphany

 Iubila, rutila, mat_er_ Eccl_es_ia:
 Nat_us_ Dei filius sugit vbera.

Florida grauida Iesse v_i_rgula;
Pep_er_it _et_ floruit v_i_rgo puerp_er_a.

 Iubila, rutila, mat_er_ Eccl_es_ia:
 Nat_us_ Dei filius sugit vbera.

Ang_e_lo docente cu_m_ stella lucida,
Reges ab oriente tulerunt mun_er_a.

 Iubila, rutila, mat_er_ Eccl_es_ia:
 Nat_us_ Dei filius sugit vbera.

Princip_es_ _et_ nobiles Arabum _et_ Saba
Suis dromedariis Madian _et_ Effa.

 Iubila, rutila, mat_er_ Eccl_es_ia:
 Nat_us_ Dei filius sugit vbera.

Qui magos conduxit luce syderea
Perducat nos ad lucem supra sydera.

Iubila, rutila, mater Ecclesia:
Natus Dei filius sugit vbera.

Amen.

14

To the Virgin

Vale, virgo Christifera,
Quem laudat mundi machina.

Vera vitis fructifera,
Vale, virgo Christifera,
Panis vite dapifera,
Quo recreatur anima.

Vale, virgo Christifera,
Quem laudat [mundi machina.]

Tollens Eue pomifera,
Vale, virgo Christifera,
Ade peccata vetera
Que diluit Ecclesia.

Vale, virgo Christifera,
Quem laudat [mundi machina.]

Porte celi clauigera,
Vale, virgo Christifera,
Paradisy meligera,
Cuncta regentis sydera.

    Vale, vi̱rgo Christi̱fera,
    Que̱m laudat [mundi machina.]

Pietate dulciflua,
Vale, vi̱rgo Christi̱fera,
Dele no̱stra facinora,
Pre̱bens ete̱rna mune̱ra.

    Vale, vi̱rgo Christi̱fera,
    Que̱m laudat mundi machina.

    Ame̱n.

Burdens 2-4, l. 2. MS. que̱m laudat &c.

15

Of the Epiphany

Cu̱m Christus nasci̱tu̱r
    De matre vi̱rgine,
Noua lux ori̱tu̱r
    In claro sydere;
A magis cerni̱tu̱r
    Tharsis e̱t Insule;
Deuote queri̱tu̱r
    Cu̱m trino mune̱re.

Regem cu̱m asserant,
    Auro Arabee,
Thus, mirra pre̱dicant
    Deu̱m in homi̱ne;
Herodis pe̱reunt
    Vires i̱n scelere,

Cum magi redeunt
   Diuino munere.

Cum hec patrata sunt,
   Completo opere,
Sua perueniunt
   Ad loca prospere.
Magos qui transtulit,
   Lucente sydere,
Luci nos inferat
   Quo non sunt tenebre.

   Amen.

16

Of Christ

   Amoris vinculo
      Nos Dei filius
         Attraxit dulciter.

Eterno seculo
   De Patre genitus,
Amoris vinculo
   Nos Dei filius,
De matris vtero
   Homo dicatus,
      Natus humiliter.

   Amoris vinculo
      Nos Dei filius
         Attraxit dulciter.

Communi stabulo
  Presepe positus,
Amoris vinculo
  Nos Dei filius,
Cum lactis pabulo
  Matris vberibus
    Pastus communiter.

    Amoris vinculo
      [Nos Dei filius
        Attraxit dulciter.]

Viuens in patulo
  Virtutum moribus,
Amoris vinculo
  Nos Dei filius,
Doctrine poculo
  Verbis operibus
    Docendo jugiter.

    Amoris vinculo
      Nos Dei [filius
        Attraxit dulciter.]

Crucis patibulo
  Pro nobis deditus,
Amoris vinculo
  Nos Dei filius
Mortis periculo
  Peccati nexibus
    Sanando peritus.

   Amoris vinculo
    Nos Dei [filius
     Attraxit dulciter.]

Celorum solio
 Paras fidelibus,
Amoris vinculo
 Nos Dei filius,
Superno premio
 Sanctorum cetibus
  Iungat feliciter.

   Amoris vinculo
    Nos Dei filius
     Attraxit dulciter.

After stanza 5: Amen.
Burden 3, ll. 2, 3. MS. &c.
Burdens 4, 5, l. 2. MS. nos Dei &c.

17

To the Virgin

 Alas, hou sholdy synge?
 Yloren is my playinge:
Hou sholdy with that olde man
To leuen and let my leman,
 Swettist of al thinge?

Succurre, mater Christi,
Menti mee tristi
Pondere peccati quo deprimitur
Prorsus ad yma semper labitur
Sine defensore.

Ortus noue lucis
Quam nobis producis
Pondere peccati sic extenuat,
Lapsos penitentes semper releuat,
Te intercessore.

Et lux illa vera
Que caritate mera
Suo splendore nos illuminat,
Celi diuo rore nos letificat,
Diuino fulgore.

Hac luce profundi
Simus et secundi;
Pie matris more nobis impetra,
Eidem coniungi virtute celica,
Superno datore.

Amen.

18

To Christ

Harrow! leo su trahy
Par fol amour de mal amy.

Jhesu, lux vera seculi,
Tui te laudant seruuli.

Gaudent videntes angeli,
Jhesu, lux vera seculi;
Pandunt melos preconii
Ob diem natale tui.

Jhesu, lux vera seculi,
Tui te laudant seruuli.

Redemptis ope subueni,
Jhesu, lux vera seculi;
Parce peccatis populi
Vita labentis fragili.

Jhesu, lux vera seculi,
Tui te laudant seruuli.

Male nos premunt emuli,
Jhesu, lux vera seculi;
Portum tanti naufragii
Da finem veri gaudii.

Jhesu, lux vera seculi,
Tui te laudant seruuli.

Amen.

19

Of the Resurrection

Haue mercie on me, frere,
Barfote that ygo.

Iam Christo moriente
   Luxit Ecclesia,
Sed ipso resurgente
   Promisit alleluya.

Vita deficiente
   Lapsa fragilia,
Ad vitam reuertente,
   Reflorent omnia.

Cruore nam rubente
   In carne fulgida
Tolluntur nostra mente
   Patrata scelera.

Persone resurgente,
   Visa presencia,
Sepulcreque patente,
   Testes sudaria.

Patente apparente,
   Palpata uulnerra,
Grataque coloquente
   Et pedum oscula.

Ad limbum descendentis
   Inferni spolia,
De morte triumphantis
   Plena victoria.

Huius solempnitatis
    Sunt hec insignia,
Vt rite celebremus
    Festa Paschalia.

Qui dedit tristi menti
    Tot grata gaudia
Det pie postulanti
    Leta perpetua.

    Amen.

20

Of the Resurrection

Resurexit Dominus;
    Cantemus alleluya.

Christus Dei filius,
Resurexit Dominus,
Pridie qui mortuus
  Surexit die tercia.

    Resurexit Dominus;
        Cantemus alleluya.

Dire morti traditus,
Resurexit Dominus,
Peccato carens penitus,
  Agnus sine macula.

    Resurexit Dominus;
        [Cantemus alleluya.]

Resplendens clamat angelus,
Resurexit Dominus;
Videndus est quantocius
   Precedens in Galilea.

    Resurexit Dominus;
    [Contemus alleluya.]

Letatus est Simon Petrus,
Resurexit Dominus,
Discipulorum cuneus,
   Visa Christi presencia.

    Resurexit Dominus;
    [Cantemus alleluya.]

Ne foret vltra dubius,
Resurexit Dominus,
Thomas dictus Didimus
   Palpauit Christi uulnera.

    Resurexit Dominus;
    [Cantemus alleluya.]

Qui in cruce positus,
Resurexit Dominus,
Cuius cruor roseus
   Lauit nostra crimina.

    Resurexit Dominus;
    [Cantemus alleluya.]

Nostre salutis baiulus,
Resurexit Dominus,
Cuius festa colimus,
   Nos ducat ad celestia.

     Amen.

Burdens 3-7, l. 2. MS. &c.

21

Of the Resurrection

Dire mortis datus pene,
Surexit die tercia.

Parans Pascha die cene,
Dire mortis datus pene,
Cibum turbe duodene
   Sedat manu propria.

   Dire mortis datus pene,
   Surexit die tercia.

Facta pace Deo plene,
Dire mortis datus pene,
Vite nostre currunt vene
   Per redimentis uulnera.

   Dire mortis datus pene,
   Surexit die tercia.

Rupta fila sunt sagene,
Dire mortis datus pene,
Hostis stricte sunt habene:
   Inferni patent spolia.

Dire mortis datus pene,
[Surexit die tercia.]

Rupte mortis sunt catene,
Dire mortis datus pene,
Vita viuit, O quam bene,
Celorum in gloria.

Dire mortis [datus pene,
Surexit die tercia.]

Orto sole tam serene,
Dire mortis datus pene,
Quod surexit Christus vere,
Gaudens clamat Ecclesia.

[Dire mortis datus pene,
Surexit die tercia.]

Ne gaudeat semiplene,
Dire mortis datus pene,
Sue iungit cantilene,
Bene sonans alleluya.

Dire mortis datus pene
Surexit die tercia.

Burden 4, l. 2. MS. &c.
Burden 5. MS. Dire mortis &c.

22

Of the Resurrection

Do, do, nightyngale synges ful myrie:
"Shal Y neure for thyn loue lengre karie."

Dies ista gaudii, die leticie:
De morte resurexit Christus hodie.

Resplendens clamat angelus, amoto lapide:
"Pridie qui mortuus est surgit de funere."

Dixit mulieribus, "Videte, dicite:
Ostendit se videntibus loco Galilee."

Apostoli gaudentes occurrunt concite;
Quem mortuum credebant viderunt viuere.

Thomas ille Didimus, nolens hoc credere,
De dubio fit solidus, palpato uulnere.

Descendit ad inferna, sed rupto carcere
Reducit ad superna redemptos sanguine.

Morti sauciatus pro nostro scelere,
A Patre coronatus est eterno munere.

Mesto qui letificat suo nomine
Ad loca nos perducat eterne glorie.

23

Of the Resurrection

En Christi fit memoria

Plangentis Christi uulnera
Mittetur vox dulcissona,
Digna dans laudum cantica.

Mutata sunt nam carmina,
Plangentis Christi uulnera,
De victa morte pristina
Cum surgit die tercia.

    Plangentis Christi uulnera
    [Mittetur vox dulcissona,
    Digna dans laudum cantica.]

Testatur vox angelica,
Plangentis Christi uulnera,
Sepulcrum et sudaria,
Mulierum oracula.

    Plangentis Christi uulnera
    [Mittetur vox dulcissona,
    Digna dans laudum cantica.]

Vera Christi presencia,
Plangentis Christi uulnera,
Pedes, manus, et latera,
Deuota pedum oscula.

    Plangentis Christi uulnera
    [Mittetur vox dulcissona,
    Digna dans laudum cantica.]

Verba, cibus, et opera,
Plangentis Christi uulnera,
Commisso clauigera
Petro datur Ecclesia.

    Plangentis Christi uulnera
    [Mittetur vox dulcissona,
    Digna dans laudum cantica.]

Decensus ad tartarea,
Plangentis Christi uulnera
Limbi patentis spolia
Reducuntur ad supera.

    Plangentis Christi uulnera
    [Mittetur vox dulcissona,
    Digna dans laudum cantica.]

Crucem passus et uulnera,
Plangentis Christi uulnera,
Vite presentis scandala
Regna in Patris gloria.

    Plangentis Christi uulnera
    [Mittetur vox dulcissona,
    Digna dans laudum cantica.]

Leta qui dat post tristicia,
Plangentis Christi uulnera,
Post vite transitoria
Nobis donet celestia.

    Plangentis Christi uulnera
    Mittetur vox dulcissona,
    Digna dans laudum cantica.

After stanza 7: amen.
Burdens 2-7, ll. 2, 3. MS. &c.

24

Of the Resurrection

Haue god day, my lemmon &c.

Resurgenti cum gloria
Gaudeat Ecclesia,
Digne cantans alleluya.

Rumpenti mortis vincula,
Resurgenti cum gloria,
Pede calcanti tartara,
Vite reddenti premia.

Resurgenti cum gloria
[Gaudeat Ecclesia,
Digne cantans alleluya.]

Visa Christi presencia,
Resurgenti cum gloria,
Multorum corda tristia
Perfusa sunt leticia.

Resurgenti cum gloria
[Gaudeat Ecclesia,
Digne cantans alleluya.]

Palpanti data uulnera,
Resurgenti cum gloria,
Beata pedum oscula,
Corda firmat incredula.

>   Resurgenti cum gloria
>   [Gaudeat Ecclesia,
>   Digne cantans alleluya.]

Qui prebes noua gaudia,
Resurgenti cum gloria,
Post vite transitoria
Dans nobis dona celestia.

>   Resurgenti cum gloria
>   [Gaudeat Ecclesia,
>   Digne cantans alleluya.]

Vt visa facie tua,
Resurgenti cum gloria,
Tecum in illa gloria
Cantemus alleluya.

>   Resurgenti cum gloria
>   [Gaudeat Ecclesia,
>   Digne cantans alleluya.]

After stanza 5: amen.
Burdens 2-6, ll. 2, 4.   MS.   &c.

25

Of Easter

>   Assunt festa Paschalia;
>   Gaudeat mater Ecclesia.

Foras procul allecia;
Assunt festa Paschalia;
Alte tonat alleluia
Agnus detur et azima.

Assunt festa Paschalia;
Gaudet mater Ecclesia.

Victa morte turpissima;
Assunt festa Paschalia;
Surexit die tercia
Christus noster cum gloria.

Assunt festa Paschalia;
[Gaudet mater Ecclesia.]

Visa Christi presencia;
Assunt festa Paschalia;
Corda gaudent amancia;
Palpantur Christi uulnera.

Assunt festa Paschalia;
[Gaudet mater Ecclesia.]

Pede calcantur tartara;
Assunt festa Paschalia;
Inferni patent spolia;
Clarescit celi ianua.

Assunt festa Paschalia
[Gaudet mater Ecclesia.]

Sedens in Patris dextera,
Assunt festa Paschalia,
Per resurgentis stigmata
Nos ducat ad celestia.

Assunt festa Paschalia;
Gaudet mater Ecclesia.

After stanza 5: amen.
Burdens 3-5, 1.2. MS. &c.

26

Of the Resurrection

Resurexit a mortuis
 Qui pridie decessit.

Nunciatur ab angelis:
Resurexit a mortuis;
Fit gaudium Christicolis,
 Cum rumor inualescit.

 Resurexit a mortuis
  Qui pridie decessit.

Comedit cum apostolis;
Resurexit a mortuis;
Manus, pedis, et lateris
 Uulnera detexit.

 Resurexit a mortuis
  Qui pridie decessit.

Regressus est ab inferis;
Resurexit a mortuis
Deductus secum spoliis
 Quo limbus expauescit.

 Resurexit a mortuis
  Qui pridie decessit.

Timor incursus credulis;
Resurexit a mortuis;
Fugatur a discipulis;
   Alleluya dulcessit.

    Resurexit a mortuis
    [Qui pridie decessit.]

Qui vitam tulit languidis,
Resurexit a mortuis,
Det illam nobis miseris
   Que finem scire nescit.

    Resurexit a mortuis
    Qui pridie decessit.

After stanza 5: amen.
Burden 5, l. 2. MS. &c.

27

Of Easter

   Dies venit, dies tua,
   In qua reflorent omnia.

Hec sunt festa Paschalia,
Dies venit, dies tua,
Nam reuiuiscunt omnia
Cum Christo die tercia.

   Die[s] venit, dies tua,
   In qua reflorent omnia.

Fugit dolor et tristia;
Dies veni, dies tua;
Virent cuncta virencia;
Vigent corda flammancia.

 Dies venit, dies tua,
 [In qua reflorent omnia.]

Inferni patent spolia;
Dies venit, dies tua;
Aperta celi ianua,
Gaudet mater Ecclesia.

 Die[s] venit, dies tua,
 [In qua reflorent omnia.]

Assunt carnes et azima;
Dies venit, dies tua;
Procul sint allecia;
Dulce canit alleluia.

 Dies venit, dies tua,
 [In qua reflorent omnia.]

Per redimentis uulnera,
Dies venit, dies tua,
Qui dedit ista munera
Donet nobis celestia.

 Dies venit, dies tua,
 In qua reflorent omnia.

  Amen.

Burdens 3-5, l. 2. MS. &c.

28

To Mary Magdalen at the Tomb

Haue merci of me, frere

Maria, noli flere
   Sepulcro Domini,
Surexit enim vere
   Sepultus ab heri.

Sepulcra patuere
   Testantur angeli;
Ad latus intuere
   Quem vocas raboni.

"Ex nunc noli lugere,"
   Dic Petro Simoni;
Tot signa claruere
   Sciant discipuli.

Qui velint me videre
   Quod sint Galilei,
Nam quod predixi vere
   Videbunt inibi.

Meruerunt me videre
   Cum cibo celebri,
Quod celi patuere
   Ascensu nobili.

Qui fecit te gaudere
   In uultu lugubri
Det secum congaudere
   Post finem seculi.

   Amen.

29

Of Christ's Wound

Languenti morbo funeris
Peccati quondam veteris
Medicina pre ceteris
Fit uulnus Christi lateris.

Cuius mixtura sanguinis
Aque diuique numinis
Cunctis medetur languidis
Adiuncto verbo iudicis.

Nam calidis et frigidis,
Siccis et ydropicis
Contractis paraliticis,
Rupturis, apostematis,

Leprosis, demoniacis,
Desperatis et mortuis,
Cunctis succurit morbidis
Empericum est hoc medicis.

Qui passus est pro miseris
Virtute sui sanguinis
Infirma nostri pectoris
Curet iungendo superis.

      Amen.

30

The World Well Lost for Christ

Gayneth me no garlond of greene,
Bot hit ben of wythoues ywroght.

Verum est quod legi satis plene
    Codice sacro volumine:
Felix est qui moritur hic bene,
    Celitus pro Christi nomine.

En fauor mundi trahit vt syrene
    Tantus sui mira dulcedine,
Sed mari mergit vt pondus arene,
    Mendici stricto examine.

Diues nam potestatis terrene
    Positus in mundi culmine
Similis est vesice vento plene
    Dum cernitur in mortis puluere.

Consultum est quod viuas hic scerene
    Celeris sublato crimine,
Vt illa loca possis dire pene
    Effugere Christi munimine.

Iudex ille qui ventilat tam plene
    Gesta, corde, visu, et opere
Post transitum vite nostre terrene
    Frui donet eterno munere.

    Amen.

31

To the Virgin

Parens partum peperisti,
    Jhesum, Dei filium.

Plaudens virgo, mater Christi,
Parens partum peperisti,
Natum mundo contulisti,
    Saluatorem omnium.

    Parens partum peperisti,
        Jhesum, Dei filium.

Nomen eius didicisti,
Parens partum peperisti,
Dum fidem angelo dedisti
    Portanti tibi nuncium.

    Parens partum peperisti,
        Jhesum, Dei filium.

Mamilla quem tu pauisti,
Parens partum peperisti,
Circumcidi voluisti
    Octaua die Dominum.

    Parens partum peperisti,
        Jhesum, Dei filium.

Vagantem aspexisti,
Parens partum peperisti,
Membra pannis inuoluisti
    Jhesum, Dei filium.

    Parens partum peperisti,
        [Jhesum, Dei filium.]

In vlnis eum tu gessisti,
Parens partum peperisti,
Sinu matris confouisti
   Regem regum omnium.

   Parens partum peperisti,
      Jhesum, [Dei filium.]

Tu que gaudens genuisti,
Parens partum peperisti,
Preserua nos a morte tristi,
   Perhenne donans gaudium.

   Parens partum peperisti,
      Jhesum, Dei filium.

         Amen.

Stanza 4, 1. 3. Membra MS. Menbra.
Burden 5, 1. 2. MS. &c.
Burden 6, 1. 2. MS. Jhesum &c.

32

Of the Nativity

   Luce qua letatur
      Mater Ecclesia,
   Deo tribuatur
      Laus et gloria.

Templo Dei sistitur
   Qui fecit sydera,
Marie de qua gignitur
   Beata viscera.

Luce qua letatur
   Mater Ecclesia,
Deo tribuatur
   Laus et gloria.

Vlnis senis suscipitur
   Qui firmat ethera;
Deo benedicitur
   Salutis gracia.

Luce qua letatur
   Mater Ecclesia,
[Deo tribuatur
   Laus et gloria.]

Salus mundi cernitur
   Et plebis gloria;
Dimitti pace petitur
   Qua gaudent funera.

Luce qua letatur
   Mater Ecclesia,
[Deo tribuatur
   Laus et gloria.]

Purificari sinitur
   Peccati nescia,
Leqique subicitur
   Sed non obnoxia.

Luce qua letatur
   Mater Ecclesia,
[Deo tribuatur
   Laus et gloria.]

Sordes qui purificat,
   Emundans omnia,
Peccato nos mundificet
   Materna gracia.

   Luce qua letatur
      Mater Ecclesia,
   [Deo tribuatur
      Laus et gloria.]

After stanza 5: Amen.
Burdens 3-5, II. 3, 4. MS. &c.

33

Of the Joy of the Church

Rutilat Ecclesia,
   Iubilat in mente:
Rutila, iubila,
   Semper attente.

Dei Patris filia,
Rutilat Ecclesia,
Dei Patris filia,
   Christum parente
Rutila, iubila,
   Semper attente.

Parit virgo regia,
Rutilat Ecclesia,
Parens virgo regia,
   Pudore manente,
Rutila, iubila,
   Semper attente.

Plaudat mundi machina,
Rutilat Ecclesia,
Plaudat mundi machina
   Puero nascente,
Rutila, iubila,
  Semper attente.

Canit vox angelica,
Rutilat Ecclesia,
Canit vox ang[e]llica,
   Pastore vidente,
Rutila, iubila,
  Semper attente.

Magi ferunt munera,
Rutilat Ecclesia,
Magi ferunt munera,
   Stella precedente,
Rutila, iubila,
  Semper attente.

Noua prebens gaudia,
Rutilat Ecclesia,
Noua prebens gaudia
   Nato redimente,
Rutila, iubila,
  Semper attente.

Perducat ad celestia,
Rutilat Ecclesia,
Perducat ad celestia
   Christo mediante,
Rutila, iubila,
  Semper attente.
     Amen.

34

Of the Nativity

"Do, do," nyghtyngale syng wel mury;
"Shal Y neure for thyn loue lengre kary."

Regem adoremus
    Superne curie;
  Matri iubilemus,
    Regine glorie.

Virgo pura carens
  Lapis rubigine,
Natum nobis parens,
  Deum in homine.

    Regem adoremus
        Superne curie;
      Matri [iubilemus,
        Regine glorie.]

Purificari voluit
  Quasi grauedine
Nos vt purificaret
  Suo iuuamine.

    Regem adoremus
        [Superne curie;
      Matri iubilemus,
        Regine glorie.]

Templo natum optulit,
    Legi Moysaice;
Tutur et columba
    Testes sunt hostie.

        Regem adoremus
            [Superne curie;
        Matri iubilemus,
            Regine glorie.]

Legem hiis qui condidit
    Diuino munere
Pro nobis se subiecit
    Legi tipice.

        Regem adoremus
            [Superne curie;
        Matri iubilemus,
            Regine glorie.]

Summo ille iustus
    Ait prophetice:
"Mundo lumen ortum,
    Salutem patrie."

        Regem adoremus
            [Superne curie;
        Matri iubilemus,
            Regine glorie.]

Que dedit nobis numen
   Tantum leticie
Ad verum ducat lumen
   Celestis patrie.

Regem adoremus
   Superne curie;
Matri iubilemus,
   Regine glorie.

After stanza 6: Amen.
Burden 3, ll. 2-4. MS. vt supra.
Burdens 4-6, ll. 2-4. MS. &c.
Stanza 6, l. 2. Tantum MS. Tantem.

35

To the Virgin

Gaude, virgo mater Christi,
Parens natum genuisti
   Cum ingenti gaudio.

Manu partum tu pauisti,
Gaude, virgo mater Christi,
Lac mamilla tu dedisti,
   Continens in gremio.

Gaude virgo mater Christi,
Parens natum genuisti
   Cum ingenti gaudio.

Natum vlnis tu gessisti,
Gaude, virgo mater Christi,
Oscula tu miscuisti
   Inflexo visus radio.

     Gaude, virgo mater Christi,
     Parens [natum genuisti
        Cum ingenti gaudio.]

Prolem pannis inuoluisti,
Gaude, virgo mater Christi,
Fassiam tu constrinxisti,
   Reclinans in stabulo.

     Gaude, virgo mater Christi,
     [Parens natum genuisti
        Cum ingenti gaudio.]

Magos tu ipsa vidisti,
Gaude, virgo mater Christi,
Adorantes ortum Christi,
   Fulgore stelle preuio.

     Gaude, virgo mater Christi,
     [Parens natum genuisti
        Cum ingenti gaudio.]

Dona regum recepisti,
Gaude, virgo mater Christi,
Que tulerunt reges isti
   Iacenti in presepio.

     Gaude, virgo mater Christi,
     [Parens natum genuisti
        Cum ingenti gaudio.]

Intelligendo concepisti,
Gaude, virgo mater Christi,
Designant honores isti
   Regi regum Domino.

   Gaude, virgo mater Christi,
   [Parens natum genuisti
      Cum ingenti gaudio.]

Tu qui gaudens peperisti,
Gaude, virgo mater Christi,
Preserua nos a morte tristi,
   Perhenni iungens premio.

   Gaude, virgo mater Ch[risti,
   Parens natum genuisti
      Cum ingenti gaudio.]

After stanza 7: Amen.
Burden 3, l. 2. MS. parens &c.
Burdens 4-7, ll. 2, 3. MS. &c.
Burden 8. The end of the first line has been cut off at the margin.
Stanza 3, l. 3. Fassiam. The m has an extra stroke in MS.

36

To Christ

Christe, redemptor omnium,
Exaudi preces supplicum.

Veni, saluator gencium,
Christe, redemptor omnium,
Cerne mundi naufragium,
Restaurans quod est perditum.

    Christe, redemptor omnium,
    Exaudi preces supplicum.

Partum nobis virgineum,
Christe, redemptor omnium,
Regem celorum, Dominum,
Effudit virgo virginum.

    Christe, redemptor omnium,
    Exaudi preces supplicum.

A Deo Patre luminum,
Christe, redemptor omnium,
Nobis mitte Paraclitum,
Illustratorem cordium.

    Christe, redemptor omnium,
    Exaudi preces supplicum.

Qui celi tenens ambitum,
Christe, redemptor omnium,
Solus ante precipium,
Perhenne dona gaudium.

Christe, redemptor omnium,
Exaudi preces supplicum.

After stanza 4: amen.

Stanza 3 is in the same hand as the rest but appears to have been added at a later time, together with marks of insertion.

After stanza 3: Qui celi &c.

37

To Christ, for Pity

Miserans, miserans,
 Parce redemptis;
Miserando iudicans,
 Parce redemptis.

Tu qui vides omnia,
Tu qui vides omnia,
Sub et supra sydera,
Sub et supra sydera.

 Miserans, miserans,
  Parce redemptis;
 Miserando iudicans,
  Parce redemptis.

Opprimitur Ecclesia,
Opprimitur Eccl[es]ia,
Que solet esse libera,
Que solet esse libera.

 Miserans, miserans,
  Parce redemptis;
 [Miserando iudicans,
  Parce redemptis.]

Crescit auaricia,
Crescit auaricia,
Dolus et malicia,
Dolus et malicia.

 Miserans, miserans,
  Parce redemptis;
 [Miserando iudicans,
  Parce redemptis.]

Amor et iusticia,
Amor et iusticia
Fugati sunt de patria,
Fugati sunt de patria.
 Miserans, miserans,
  Parce redemptis;
 [Miserando iudicans,
  Parce redemptis.]

Vigent vbique spolia,
Vigent vbique spolia,
Liuor et incendia,
Liuor et incendia.

 Miserans, miserans,
  Parce redemptis;
 [Miserando iudicans,
  Parce redemptis.]

Qui iudicabis singula,
Qui iudicabis singula,
Reges et imperia,
Reges et imperia,

  Miserans, miserans,
   Parce redemptis;
  [Miserando iudicans,
   Parce redemptis.]

Presenti de miseria,
Presenti de miseria,
Perduc nos ad supera,
Perduc nos ad supera.

  Miserans, miserans,
   Parce redemptis;
  Miserando iuicans,
   Parce redemptis.

Burden 3, II. 3, 4. MS. vt supra.
Burdens 4-7, II. 3, 4. MS. &c.

38

To Christ, on His Epiphany

  Jhesu, lux vera mencium,
  Serua tuum peculium.

Reges Saba et Arabum,
Jhesu, lux vera mencium,
Et multitudo dromedum
Te querunt natum puerum.

  Jhesu, lux vera mencium,
  Serua tuum peculium.

57

Dono te trium munerum,
Jhesu, lux vera mencium,
Secundum sensum misticum
Tuum laudant preconium.

 Jhesu, lux vera mencium,
 Serua tuum peculium.

Thure Deum altissumum,
Jhesu, lux vera mencium,
Auro regem et dominum,
Sed mirra mortis gremium.

 Jhesu, lux vera mencium,
 Serua tuum peculium.

Lumen stelle perfulgidum,
Jhesu, lux vera mencium,
Ne declinent in deuium,
Ducatum prebet preuium.

 Jhesu, lux vera mencium,
 Serua tuum peculium.

Lumen qui das sydereum,
Jhesu, lux vera mencium,
Magos ducens ad volitum,
Duc nos ad lumen luminum.

 Jhesu, lux vera mencium,
 Serua tuum peculium.

  Amen.

39

Of Christ's Baptism

Nouum lumen apparuit,
   Quo vera lux clarescit.

Ad orientem patuit,
Nouum lumen apparuit,
Natum regem edocuit
  Et magos antecessit.

   Nouum lumen apparuit,
     Quo vera lux clarescit.

Ad orandum se prebuit,
Nouum lumen apparuit,
Presepe non abhorruit
  Qui totum mundum rexit.

   Nouum lumen apparuit,
     Quo vera lux clarescit.

Qui baptizari voluit,
Nouum lumen apparuit,
Virtutem aquis tribuit
  Qua anima pulcrescit.

   Nouum lumen apparuit,
     Quo vera lux clarescit.

Paterna vox intonuit,
Nouum lumen apparuit,
Testis de celo sonuit
  Quod filium dilexit.

   Nouum lumen apparuit,
     Quo vera lux clarescit.

Dum nupciis interfuit,
Nouum lumen apparuit,
Aquam in vinum transtulit
   Quod in ore dulcessit.

  Nouum lumen apparuit,
    Quo vera lux clarescit.

Qui nobis nasci voluit,
Nouum lumen apparuit,
Det vitam quam optulit
   Que nusquam euanescit.

  Nouum lumen apparuit,
    Quo vera lux clarescit.

    Amen.

40

Of the Presentation in the Temple

  Heu, alas, par amour,
   Qy moy myst en taunt dolour.

Vale, mater virgo pura,
Tu et tua genitura,
Tuum natum offertura
   Templo Ierosolimis.

Subiecta licet nos sis legi,
Placens tamen Summo Regi,
Natum offers templi gregi,
   Dei simul et hominis.

Quem suscepit Simon ille,
Deo carus plus quam mille,
Cuius verba sunt suttile
    Fascis diui numinis.

Mundi lumen in quid cerno,
Salutem gentis de superno,
Pacem petit ab externo,
    Nunc indictam mortuis.

Impuritatem tu que nescis,
Puris tamen data cum sis,
Purificari quomodo scis,
    Immunis ab exteris.

Natus tuus, legis lator,
Adimpleuit vt amator,
Exemplum dat verbi sator
    Derelinquens aliis.

Lumen verum matris prece,
Seruans quam ab omni fece,
Preserua nos a tristi nece,
    Coniunge Christicolis.

    Amen.

41

Of the Nativity

Hey, how, the cheualdoures wokes al nyght

En parit virgo regia,
En parit virgo regia,
Maria plena gracia,
Maria plena gracia.

In vtero sanctificata,
Ab angelo dum nunciata,
Spiritu Sancto inpregnata,
   Deum parit in homine.

   En parit virgo regia,
   En parit virgo regia,
   Maria plena gracia,
   Maria plena gracia.

Parit mater virgo pura
Et post partum permansura,
Felix illa genitura,
   Sine viri semine.

   En parit virgo regia,
   [En parit virgo regia,
   Maria plena gracia,
   Maria plena gracia.]

Testantur hoc Ysayas,
Dauid Rex et Jeremias,
Micheas et Zacharyas,
   In prophetarum ordine.

   En parit virgo regia,
   [En parit virgo regia,
   Maria plena gracia,
   Maria plena gracia.]

Partus iste nobis datus
Et pro nobis immolatus,
Nostri moras incolatus
   Claudat beatitudine.
         Amen.

Burden 3, ll. 2-4. MS. vt supra.
Burden 4, ll. 2-4. MS. &c.

42

Of the Circumcision

Jhesu bone, Jhesu pie,
Jhesu fili, flos Marie,
Circumcisus ista die
    Pro nobis mundi miseris.

Nomen tuum salutare
Dat scriptura causam quare,
Nam tu venisti nos saluare,
    Salus in angustiis.

Quem adorant magi reges,
Pastores pascentes greges,
Testantur scientes leges
    Ex libris propheticis.

Que genuisti Saluatorem,
Ducem nostrum et pastorem,
Et a morte redemptorem,
    Ade peccati veteris.

Per tui nati sanctum ortum
Duc nos ad salutis portum,
Quo nil graue, nichil tortum,
    Sed semper frui superis.

    Amen.

43

To God

Summe Deus clemencie,
Mundique factor machine.

Trino sumus certamine,
Summe Deus clemencie:
Mundi, carnis, cum demone,
Iterque nostrum fragile.

Summe Deus clemencie,
Mundique factor machine.

Rectorque noster, aspice,
Summe Deus clemencie;
Vitam et mores corrige,
Viamque pacis dirige.

Summe Deus clemencie,
Mundique factor machine.

Memento nostri, Domine,
Summe Deus clemencie,
Vt dono tue gracie
Preserues nos a crimine.

Summe Deus clemencie,
[Mundi factor machine.]

Vi mortis tue viuide,
Summe Deus clemencie,
Calcato tartaro pede,
Hostem vicisti strenue.

Summe Deus clemencie
[Mundique factor machine.]

Ab hoste tu nos protege,
Summe Deus clemencie,
In hora mortis suscipe,
Et omni salua tempore.

Burdens 4, 5, 1. 2. MS. &c.

44

To Christ

Scandenti supra sidera,
Locato Patris dextera,
Laus, honor sit, et gloria.

Vincenti tanta prelia,
Scandenti supra sidera,
Celestia, terestria,
Nutu fatentur subdita.

    Scandenti supra sidera,
    [Locato Patris dextera,
    Laus, honor sit, et gloria.]

Comestione preuia,
Scandenti supra sidera,
Pandit iter per ethera
Ne caro fiat dubia.

    Scandenti supra sidera,
    [Locato Patris dextera,
    Laus, honor sit, et gloria.]

Videntes hoc magnalia,
Scandenti supra sidera,
Tollunt ad celos lumina
Quem cepit nubes fulgida.

    Scandenti supra sidera,
    [Locato Potris dextera,
    Laus, honor sit, et gloria.]

Testatur vox angelica,
Scandenti supra sidera,
Iudicaturum omnia
Venturum hunc per aera.

    Scandenti supra sidera,
    [Locato Potris dextera,
    Laus, honor sit, et gloria.]

Tenens libram et pondera,
Scandenti supra sidera,
Nobis remittat scelera,
Secum ducens ad supera.

    Amen.

Burdens 2, 3, II. 2, 3.   MS. &c.

45

To the Holy Spirit

O Deus, Sancte Spiritus,
Summi dulcoris alitus.

Duorum amor medius,
O Deus, Sancte Spiritus,
Verus noster Paraclitus
Et consolator intimus.

    O Deus, Sancte Spiritus,
    Summi dulcoris alitus.

Dextre Dei tu digitus,
O Deus, Sancte Spiritus,
Bonorum dator optimus,
Linguarum sator celitus.

    O Deus, Sancte Spiritus,
    [Summi dulcoris alitus.]

Lumen infundens sencibus,
O Deus, Sancte Spiritus,
Corda demulcens penitus,
Vrens amoris fascibus.

    O Deus, Sancte Spiritus,
    [Summi dulcoris alitus.]

Pacis autor egregius,
O Deus, Sancte Spiritus,
Dator, amator inclitus,
Assistens postulantibus.

    [O Deus, Sancte Spiritus,
    Summi dulcoris alitus.]

Qui das salutem gentibus,
O Deus, Sancte Sp[irit]us,
Mestis solamen mentibus,
Aurem da nostris precibus.

 O Deus, Sancte Sp[irit]us,
 [Summi dulcoris alitus.]

Hostem repellas longius,
O Deus, Sancte Spiritus,
Pacem da nostris cordibus,
Iungendo celi ciuibus.

 Amen.

46

Of the Holy Spirit

Spiritus Sancti gracia,
In quo clarescunt omnia,
Nobis assit per secula.

Dudum sacrata pectora,
Spiritus Sancti gracia,
Cor, linguam, et labia
Lingua repleuit ignea.

 Spiritus Sancti gracia,
 In quo clarescunt omnia,
 Nobis assit per secula.

Fantur Dei magnalia,
Sp[irit]us Sancti gracia,
Linguarum cuncta genera
Cum admiracione nimia.

> Spiritus Sancti gracia,
> In quo clarescunt omnia,
> Nobis assit per secula.

Iudea tunc incredula,
Spiritus Sancti gracia,
Discip[u]lorum agmina
Repleta dicit crapula.

> Spiritus Sancti gracia,
> In quo clarescunt omnia,
> Nobis assit per secula.

Petrus virtute celica,
Spiritus Sancti gracia,
Pulsa tanta vesania,
Facta docet prophetica.

> Spiritus Sancti gracia,
> In quo clarescunt omnia,
> Nobis assit per secula.

Qui sc[i]t et potest omnia,
Spiritus Sancti gracia,
Det nunc quieta tempora
Et post eterna gaudia.

> Amen.

47

Of the Nativity

Canite, canite, uultu iocundo,
Canite, canite, uultu iocundo,
> Nato Domino;

Iubilando psallite cantu rotundo,
Iubilando psallite cantu rotund[o]
   Marie filio.

Canite, canite, mente decora,
Canite, canite, mente decora
   Nato Domino;
Iubilando psallite vice sonora,
Iubilando psallite vice sonora
   Marie filio.

Canite, canite, voce fecunda,
Canite, canite, voce fecunda
   Nato Domino;
Iubilando psallite mente letabunda,
Iubilando psallite mente letabunda
   Marie filio.

Canite, canite, puero nascenti,
Canite, canite, puero nascenti,
   Nato Domino;
Iubilando psallite natum parienti,
Iubilando psallite natum parienti,
   Marie filio.

Canite, canite, regi angelorum,
Canite, canite, regi angelorum,
   Nato Domino;
Vt pie canenti de regna polorum,
Vt pie canenti de regna polorum,
   Marie filio.

Stanza 1, ll. 4, 5. Iubilando] MS. Iubilande.
Stanza 2, l. 2. decora] MS. decoro.
        l. 5. sonora] MS. sornora.

48

Of the Nativity

De sole rutilo sol alter oritur,
Sic mundo geminus sol superfunditur,
Sic ignis celitus in terram mittitur,
Sic mundi scoria vetus exuritur.

Sol sole grauidus iuxta nos queritur,
Et mundus ignibus vicinis vritur,
Set tanta glacies in duram vertitur
Cristalli speciem nec estu soluitur.

Venter eburneus, venter mirificus,
Mundo mirifico fit meconomicus;
Contentus continens quod mundus ciclicus
Non cladit vterus includit modicus.

Fit magnus paruulus, seruus et dominus,
Contentus continens, breuis interminus;
Antiqu[u]s nascitur, distansque comminus,
Excelsus humilis et simplex geminus.

Vagit puerulus et mammas paruulis
Contractat manibus atque digitulis;
Iunguntur sepius inpressis osculis
Materna filii labia labellis.

O Dei genitrix, O gemma virginum,
Que prolem suscipis a patre luminum,
Tu nos a fecibus deteros criminum
Transfer ad supera post vite terminum.

Stanza 3, l. 3. ciclucus] MS. ciclitus
Stanza 5, 2. 4. labia] MS. labra.

Of the Annunciation

Salutat angelus blande iuuenculam,
Virgo post modicum offert ancillulam;
Verbum inueniens puellam credulam
In ventrem labitur per codis semitam.

Verbum virgineum in uentrem properat,
Vbi celestia terrenis federat;
Dulci pondustulo puellam onerat,
Nec tum virginis florem obliquitat.

Inpregnat virginis verbum ventriculum,
Nec pudicicie soluit signaculum;
Verbum in virgine iam factum verbulum,
Novellum inchoat in ventre lectulum.

In ventre simul sunt lictum et deitas,
Fictor, fictile, maiestas, paruitas,
Altum et humile, limis sublimitas,
Firmum et fragile, virtus, infirmitas.

Profert virgenea gleba gramisculum,
In cuius adipe est mentis pabulum;
Qui pascit volucres per terre circulum
Per mamme pascitur beatum frustulum.

O virgo nobilis, O plena gracia !
Diuinis imbribus vbertim rorida,
Riga per graciam que vides arida,
Et transfer lugubres ad regna placida.

Amen.

Stanza 5, l. 1. virginea] MS. virgenea.

50

Of the Sound of Jesus' Name

Verbum virgineum inpregnans vterum,
Jhesus vocatum est a patre luminum,
Habens signifere nomen preconium
Quo genu flectitur funda demonum.

Cum Jhesum audio natumque virginis,
Vel sacris lectito scriptum in paginis,
Sonus et litera sacri vocaminis
Pastu me recreant mire dulcedinis.

Cum nati virginis Jhesus depromitur,
Aer salubrior fit qui percutitur,
Et melle mulcior ad aures labitur,
Cum sonus melleus per eum vehitur.

Cum aures percutit Jhesu prolacio,
Statim affectuum tota colleccio;
In vnum cogitur, et cum tripudio
Occurrit nomini leta processio.

Cum auri melleus sonus infunditur,
Mens quam vis ferrea tota resoluitur;
Cum auris timpanum hoc sono tangitur,
Inclinans obuiam sono progreditur.

Explorat igitur auris angustias
Vt sacras colligat Jhesu reliquias,
Et signas inuenit dulces minuceas,
Has plus quam Darii probat diuicias.

Mariam inuoco, que flos est virginum,
Que gaudens genuit Jhesum saluificum;
A nato postulet nobis mirificum
Vt donet gaudium non habens terminum.

Stanza 1, l. 1.   inpregnans] MS. inprengnans.
Stanza 2, l. 3.   vocaminis] MS. vocaminus.

51

Of the Flight into Egypt

Magi repatriant post data munera,
Non ea qua venerant via sed altera,
Set Jhesus remanet pendens ad ubera
Que profert paruulo viro puerpera.

Ad sua redeunt magi celeriter,
Herodem fugiunt, qui furit fortiter,
Set Jhesus remanet, videte qualiter:
logatur paruulus cum matre dulciter.

Maria paruulo girat corpusculum,
Nunc genas osculans, nunc os, nunc collulum,
Manus, brachiola, pectus, dorsiculum,
Latus et humeros, pedem, geniculum.

Crescit puerulus qui magnitudine
Par Deo creditur et celcitudine;
Herodes metuit audito nomine
Regis qui proditur stelle vibramine.

Herodes perfidus ne regni gloria
Priuetur metuit et cum versuscia
Spondens obsequium occulta odia,
Sic blandis tegitur verbis rancordia.

In fontes laceras leo teribilis;
Truncatur turmula tenella fragilis;
Clamor in Betheleem crebrescit flebilis:
In Rama resonat vox lamentabilis.

Oportet igitur Iosep sanctissime
Egiptum petere festinantissime,
Grassatur impius rex inmanissime,
De morte paruuli tracans cautissime.

Iosep antiquitus exponens sompnium
Nam cisti meruit regni dominium;
Egipte, suscipe nunc Iosep alium
Qui tibi geminat solis exennium.

Egiptum adiens prosternit idola;
Qui mentis tenebras fugat et odia
Det nobis omnibus post vite tedia
Cum celi ciuibus petiri gloria.

        Ame[n].

Stanza 3, l. 1. corpusculum] MS. corpisculum.
Stanza 3, l. 2. nunc] MS. ninc.
Stanza 8, l. 1. sompnium] MS. sompinum.

52

Of the Bread of Life

Maria decoquit panem saluificum
In ventris clibano per ignem misticum,
Panem dulcissimum set tamen modicum
Quo totum reficit conuentum celicum.

Hic panis coquitur celesti facula,
Factus de virginis pura farimia,
Nec panem vstulat conburens flammula,
Nec pastam polluit polluta pinsula.

Inmundus clibanus igne non caluit,
Nec pastam sordidus contactus polluit,
Set Dei digitus farinam miscuit,
Et quod confectum est hic pastor pinsuit.

Nostra panifica panem distribuit,
Qui zima veteri nunquam coacuit;
Hoc pane pastus est quicumque voluit:
Solus ieiunus est qui pastum renuit.

Hunc panem frangimus et tamen fraccio
Eius qui frangitur non est particio;
Hunc panem sumimus, et tamen sumpcio
Eius qui sumitur non est consumpcio.

Per panes alios fames depellitur,
Set tamen aspera sitis non tollitur;
Set quisquis virginis pane reficitur
Nec famem anxiam nec sitim patitur.

Celestes etenim ciues esuriunt,
Sed in esurie penam non senciunt,
Nam panem commedunt et panem cupiunt,
Ingendi gaudio bibunt et siciunt.

Felix conuiuium, felix refeccio,
In qua virgineus panis est pastio,
Quo nos reficiat suo conuiuio,
Qui solus saciat sine fastidio.

        Amen.

Stanza 1, l. 1. decoquit] MS. docoquit.
Stanza 5, l. 3. sumimus] MS. summimus.

53

Of the Virgin's Motherhood

Stupens intueor ventrem Christifore,
Ventrosam feminam sed sine venere,
    Non prodigio;
Celestem celica virgo dulcedine
Partum illaqueat et pulcritudine
    Sub carnis pallio.

Concepit, peperit, intacta masculum,
Que nunquam masculi sencis opusculum,
    Virtute celica;
Sic Deum efficit nostrum fraterculum
Nostra sororcula per carnis sacculum,
    Beata viscera.

Virgo verbigena, felix nutricula,
Mater ancillula, nota sororcula,
   Sine lacinia !
Magnum in modica claudit domuncula,
Et totum tunicat carnis particula,
   Beata sarcina.

Conuertit genitor in matrem filiam,
Antiquis prosilit ad puericiam
   In paruo spacio;
Nouam ingreditur rex regum regiam,
Nec vllam virgini fecit iniuriam
   Ventrali modio.

O fons dulcedinis, O mater inclita !
O via luminis, O vite semita !
   O stella splendida !
Tu nos in lectulo doloris visita,
Et transfer lugubres ad regna lucida
   In lucis orbita.

   Amen.

Stanza 1, l.1. Christifere] MS. Christifore.

54

To the Virgin

O Dei genitrix, cui nulla similis,
Preit vel sequitur, virgo tam humilis,
   O plena gracia !
Porta tu miseris semper adhibilis,
Presta quod expedit tuis Christicolis
   In vite semita.

Tu summi principis turnus eburneus,
Thorale roseum et chorus floreus,
    Fenustra celica !
Inpenetrabilis in bello clipeus,
In quo credencium tutatur cuneus,
    O fenix vnica !

In ignis innocuis in rubo rutilat,
Nec rubum nubulo fumali nubilat
    In ignis incendio;
Deus puellule secreta visitat,
In ventre virginis simplex se duplicat
    Nouo miraculo.

Virgo languencium medela concita,
Solue quos criminum innodat cordula,
    Complana tumida;
Enoda nodulos, et funes ruptita
Quibus astringimur, iacentes releua,
    Deduc ad supera.

    Amen.

55

Of the Virgin

Consendit Salamon ventrale ferculum,
Nec pudici[ci]e soluit signaculum
    Tactu femineo;
Venter eburneus producit masculum
Per quem redimitur optatum seculum
    Partu virgineo.

Ardere cernitur ardenti radio
Rubus nec vritur ignis incendio
    Visu Moysayco;
Sic nec corumpitur suscepto filio
Virgo nec leditur in puerperio
    Rore deifico.

In ventre virginis cubat leunculus
Qui suis dentibus non est mordaculus,
    Rugitus tollitur;
Iam enim factus est agnus agniculus
Modere renuens eius denticulus
    Mamillis pascitur.

O virgo regia, O virgo nobilis !
Que Deum concipis et nobis parturis
    Diuino munere;
Tuis Christicolis deposse miseris,
Post vite tedia nos frui superis
    Eterno lumine.

        Amen.

Stanza 1, l. 3.   femineo] MS. fomineo.
Stanza 4, l. 3.   munere]   MS. munero.

56

Of the Nativity

Maria virgo gen[u]it
    Manentem supra sidera;
Mamillam ori prebuit
    Sua sugenti vbera.

Pro nobis nasci voluit;
Precepe non abhoruit.

Vagit infans inter arta,
    Conditus presepia;
Membra pannis inuoluta
    Stric[t]a sunt cum fascia.

Lacte natum aluit
Per quem nec alis esurit.

Angelorum consorcio
    Vox alta laude sonnuit;
Pastorum contubernio
    Vie ducatum prebuit.

Pacemque nobis cecinit,
Viamque pacis dirigit.

O virgo mater nobilis,
    Qui credidisti nuncio,
Perfecta sunt in omnibus
    Que dicta sunt ab angelo.

Beata sit que genuit,
Que vitam nobis tribuit.

57

Of the Nativity

Laudet cor Deo deditum
Diuinum natalicium:
Non habet laudis terminum
Tanti festi preconium.

Laudemus et nos filium,
Nostre salutis baiulum:
Gaudet chorus celestium
Pro salute fidelium.

Sit nostri festi gaudium
Qui est futurus premium.

58

To Christ

O verbum Dei filius,
    Deus origine,
Caro factum, humanatus,
    De matre virgine.

Caritatis cumulus,
    Mira dulcedine,
Quod frater noster factus es,
    Attraxit hodie.

Angelici te laudant
    Super curie,
Pacemque nobis nunciant,
    Dei cum homine.

Fac digne te laudemus
    Pro tanto munere:
Letemur, iubilemus,
    Verbo et opere.

Nam fas non est inter nos
    Locus tristicie
Dum salus nobis oritur,
    Fons vite venie.

Nobis qui te dedisti
   Valle miserie,
Duc nos de loco tristi
   Ad vitam glorie.

59

Of the Nativity

Caritate nimia nos Deo diligente
   Letemur hodie.
Nato Dei filio de matre pariente
   Letemur hodie.
Verbum caro factum est, angelo docente,
   Letemur hodie.
De pace nobis data cum angelo canente
   Letemur hodie.
Deus humanatus est, pastore vidente:
   Letemur hodie.
A magis adoratus est, stella precedente:
   Letemur hodie.
Qui magos attraxit, sidere fulgente,
   Letemur hodie,
Ad celum nos transferat, Christo perducente:
   Letemur hodie.

60
Of the Error of the World

Videbitis qualis et quantus mundi sit error in illecebris.

    Rectores habentes greges,
    Pomposi qui condunt leges,
        Vbi iam sunt?
    Quorum gesta quia fuerunt
        In latebris
    Velud funesta nunc perierunt
        In tenebris.

Videbitis qualis et quantus [mundi sit error in illecebris.]

    Multi reges ante fuerunt
    Mundi passus qui transsierunt--
        Vbi iam sunt?
    Granes et ossa putressentes
        In delubris,
    Spiritus et anime uultu gementes
        Cum miseris.

Videbitis qualis et quantus [mundi sit error in illecebris.]

    Consultum est qui sunt venientes,
    De se ipsis sint cogitantes--
        Vbi iam sun[t?]
    Vt tuti, securi, atque defensi
        De lugubris:
    Erecti sint et congaudentes
        Cum superis.

Videbitis qualis et quantus [mundi sit error in illecebris.]

Burden 3. MS. Videbitis qualis et quantis &c.
Burden 4.   Videbitis qualis et et quantis &c.
Stanza 3, l. 3.   The last letter is cut off at the margin.

INDEX OF FIRST LINES

	No.	Page	MS.f (or ff.)
Ab alto diuini culminis	10	14	71 r.
Ad orientem patuit	39	59	74 v.
Canite, canite, uultu iocundo	47	69	75 v.
Caritate nimia nos Deo diligente	59	83	77 r.
Christi parentele	12	17	71 r.
Christus Dei filius	20	28	72 r.
Consendit Salamon ventrale ferculum	55	79	76 v.
Cuius forti potencia	7	10	70 v.
Cuius nomen est Qui Est	1	1	70 r.
Cum Christus nascitur	15	21	71 v.
Da, da nobis nunc	9	12	70 v.
De sole rutilo sol alter oritur	48	71	75 v.
Dei Patris filia	33	46	73 v.
Dies ista gaudii, die leticie	22	32	72 r.
Dudum sacrata pectora	46	68	75 v.
Duorum amor medius	45	67	75 r. and v.
Eterno seculo	16	22	71 v.
Florida grauida lesse virgula	13	19	71 r.
Foras procul allecia	25	36	72 v.
Gaudent videntes angeli	18	26	71 v.
Grata Deo tue gene	6	9	70 v.
Hec sunt festa Paschalia	27	39	73 r.
Iam Christo moriente	19	27	71 v., 72 r.
In vtero santificata	41	61	74 v., 75 r.
Jhesu bone, Jhesu pie	42	63	75 r.
Languenti morbo funeris	29	42	73 r.
Laudet cor Deo deditum	57	81	77 r.
Laus Christo reginato	8	11	70 v.

	No.	Page	MS.f (or ff.)
Magi repatriant post data munera	51	74	76 r.
Manu partum tu pauisti	35	51	74 r.
Maria decoquit panem saluificum	52	76	76 r. and v.
Maria, noli flere	28	41	73 r.
Maria virgo genuit	56	80	76 v., 77 r.
Menti mee tristi	3	4	70 r.
Mutata sunt nam carmina	23	32	72 r. and v.
Nunciatur ab angelis	26	38	72 v., 73 r.
O Dei genitrix, cui nulla similis	54	78	76 v.
O verbum Dei filius	58	82	77 r.
Parans Pascha die cena	21	30	72 r.
Peperit virgo	11	15	71 r.
Plaudens virgo, mater Christi	31	44	73 v.
Rectores habentes greges	60	84	77 r.
Reges Saba et Arabum	38	57	74 v.
Rumpenti mortis vincula	24	35	72 v.
Salutat angelus blande iuuenculam	49	72	75 v., 76 r.
Sine viri semine	2	2	70 r.
Stude Christo psallere	5	7	70 v.
Stupens intueor ventrem Christifore	53	77	76 v.
Succurre, mater Christi	17	24	71 v.
Templo Dei sistitur	32	45	73 v.
Trino sumus certamine	43	64	75 r.
Tu qui vides omnia	37	55	74 r. and v.
Vale, mater virgo pura	40	60	74 v.
Veni, saluator gencium	36	54	74 r.
Vera vitis fructifera	14	20	71 r.
Verbo rerum principio	4	5	70 r.
Verbum virgineum inpregnans vterum	50	73	76 r.

	No.	Page	MS.f (or ff.)
Verum est quod legi satis plene	30	43	73 v.
Vincenti tanta prelia	44	65	75 r.
Virgo pura carens	34	49	74 r.

www.ingramcontent.com/pod-product-compliance
Lightning Source LLC
Chambersburg PA
CBHW050817090426

42736CB00022B/3479